Lauren is an ama⎡⎦ ⎡⎦ ⎡⎦ ome much through her faith in Je⎡⎦ ⎡⎦ Christ. She is a dear friend of mine, and I admire how she views fears and the way she sees beauty. So much to learn from!

BETHANY HAMILTON
Pro surfer and author of *Soul Surfer*

I love it! This is a must-read for any young woman who desires confidence and authenticity. I was captivated by the real-life stories and was drawn into a clearer picture of what God truly cares about in each one of us—our heart! *Your Beautiful Heart* delivers an intimate look at God's view of true beauty. Readers will definitely grow closer to God through these pages.

SUSIE SHELLENBERGER
Speaker and author; SusieShellenberger.com

Get a copy of *Your Beautiful Heart* and prepare to be changed! You are about to become breathtakingly beautiful—the never-fading, always-glowing beauty that's rooted in the truth of God's love. Lauren's fresh approach will prove that outer appearance does not define true beauty. It is all about your heart, the person you are on the inside. So get reading! As Lauren's words and the Holy Spirit work together, your heart will become more beautiful, more loving, more forgiving, more free, more others-focused, more . . . well, just dive in. You'll see what I mean.

ANDREA STEPHENS
Author and founder of The B.A.B.E. Event: Beautiful, Accepted, Blessed, Eternally Significant

With grace, authenticity, and depth, Lauren shares her life in *Your Beautiful Heart*. She is a powerful voice in our culture, confidently leading young women down a path of true beauty and identity that is grounded in our identity in Christ. God is using Lauren in a powerful, culture-shifting way, and her impact on young women is making ripples that will last for generations to come.

KAT HARRIS
Photographer and founder of *The Refined Woman* blog

Lauren is an example of how God's beauty shines best from brokenness. Her courage to share her story, paired with Lisa's gift of writing, makes this an excellent resource for young women. It is also a great tool for youth leaders who want their students to experience what real beauty is.

LAURIE POLICH SHORT
Speaker and author of *Finding Faith in the Dark*

your beautiful heart

your *beautiful* heart

31 reflections on love, faith, friendship, and becoming a girl who shines

lauren scruggs
with lisa velthouse

TYNDALE
MOMENTUM

An Imprint of
Tyndale House Publishers, Inc.

Visit Tyndale online at www.tyndale.com.

Visit Tyndale Momentum online at www.tyndalemomentum.com.

TYNDALE, Tyndale Momentum, and the Tyndale Momentum logo are registered trademarks of Tyndale House Publishers, Inc. Tyndale Momentum is an imprint of Tyndale House Publishers, Inc.

Your Beautiful Heart: 31 Reflections on Love, Faith, Friendship, and Becoming a Girl Who Shines

Designed by Jacqueline L. Nuñez

Published in association with the literary agency of WordServe Literary Agency, www.wordserveliterary.com.

Library of Congress Cataloging-in-Publication Data

Scruggs, Lauren.
    Your beautiful heart : 31 reflections on love, faith, friendship, and becoming a girl who shines / Lauren Scruggs, with Lisa Velthouse.
        pages cm
    Includes bibliographical references.
    ISBN 978-1-4143-7671-4 (sc)
1. Teenage girls—Religious life. 2. Christian girls—Religious life. 3. Beauty, Personal—Religious aspects—Christianity. 4. Self-perception in adolescence—Religious aspects—Christianity. I. Title.
    BV4551.3.S37 2015
    248.8'33—dc23   2014039389

Printed in the United States of America

21   20   19   18   17   16   15
7   6   5   4   3   2   1

To all the women in my life who have shown me real beauty.
Thank you for putting God's love on display.

Contents

Your Heart for Others

Your Distinctive Heart

Your Heart Looking Forward

Foreword

by Jason Kennedy

When I saw Lauren for the first time, two things stood out to me most.

The first was her confidence . . . and the second was her smile.

It was in the studio at *E!News*, where I work as a host. Lauren was there to do an interview with Giuliana Rancic about her accident. I had heard about Lauren and the tragedy that had taken her left eye and hand. As I watched her talk in person, laughing and sharing her story, I could tell: This is someone *real*. At the time, Lauren was in the thick of recovery, facing insecurities and uncertainties—but she was finding the confidence to put herself out there because she knew it could help others. You couldn't miss how beautiful that was.

And even from across the studio, I noticed her smile. It was one of those smiles that, even on your worst day, would make you feel better. After such a terrible accident, Lauren could have chosen *not* to smile and to view the world with bitterness and pain. And yet she was smiling. I wanted to get to know the woman behind that smile.

That was our beginning. We went hiking with her mom and my friend the next day. Lauren lived in Dallas and I live in California, but we continued to talk or Skype every day afterward. I came to love Lauren because she is funny, smart, sweet, and considerate of everyone around her. She is thoughtful, always up for an adventure, and fits right in with the family and friends who are important to me. And she's quirky—it makes me laugh that she keeps four different packs of gum in her purse at all times, just in case.

But what makes her truly beautiful to me is her heart, and that's what you'll see on the pages of this book. We all have things we feel anxious about, things we wish we could change about our bodies or our personalities. Lauren is no different, but she doesn't let those things hold her back, because ultimately she knows who she is in Christ. As you read *Your Beautiful Heart*, your heart will become centered in God's love for you. You'll discover confidence, true beauty, and the courage to smile. Lauren cares so deeply for others, and it's because she cares for you that she's written this book. *Your Beautiful Heart* is a message straight from Lauren's heart to yours. I'm so glad you're not missing it.

I've always been moved by Lauren's story. She's been through so much, and her whole life changed on the day of her accident. But then I think, *So did mine.* Without that day, I never would have met her, seen her gorgeous smile, or known her beautiful heart. I never would have filled her apartment with white tulips and lit candles outside her balcony that spelled "Will you marry me?" I don't know why God chose this path for us, but I can't help but be grateful that I got that chance to propose, that Lauren said yes, and that I will be able to spend the rest of my life with a woman who is truly beautiful—not just on the outside, but in every way that matters most.

Introduction
An Imprint for Your Heart

"*B*eauty is on the inside." I've believed this for as long as I can remember, but it wasn't until recently that I began to grasp the magnificent, powerful, gut-wrenching depth of what it means.

In December 2011, I was in an accident. I was hit in the head, the hand, and the shoulder by the spinning propeller of a small plane. That accident changed how I look. It literally dug into my looks: denting the top of my skull, cutting off my left hand, and slicing down the front of my face, eventually leaving me without one of my eyes. I have scars and prostheses now. I needed hair extensions for a while.

I'm not going to waste your time or mine pretending those physical changes were easy to handle. They weren't. After my accident, it took a while before I could look at myself in a full-length mirror. When I finally did, I sobbed.

Maybe you would've sobbed too, and maybe for some of the same reasons I did. One reason I was so upset is that sometimes I have a warped and messed-up understanding of beauty. Maybe sometimes your understanding of beauty is warped and messed-up too.

Every day, you and I are bombarded from multiple directions by a giant beauty lie. This false message often comes at us from Hollywood's movie reels and New York's editorial pages, sure—but it wouldn't be fair to blame the entertainment industry alone. We hear the lie being spoken from the mouths of our friends, our peers, and sometimes even our parents. And we hear it whispered from the quiet and secret places in our own individual hearts too.

Here is the lie:
A certain kind of physical appearance equals beauty.

The word *equals* in that sentence isn't an accident. In many ways our world has turned beauty into a basic math equation, where figuring out how beautiful you are is as simple as adding up a column of numbers. The "right" physical features are like positive numbers, and the "wrong" physical features are like negatives. All you have to do is tally up your personal positives and subtract your negatives, and you'll know how beautiful (or not beautiful) you are.

We don't have to look very long or very hard to see this kind of beauty-math at work all around us. It's a painfully familiar system. In fact, I bet you can identify our world's beauty standards just as easily as I can. Take a look at the list below—isn't this how it goes?

Face? Symmetrical.
Lips? Plump.
Nose? Straight and narrow.
Teeth? Straight and white.
Skin? Smooth and clear.
Eyes? Big, with long, thick lashes.
Cheekbones? High.
Hair? Full and face-framing.
Jawline? Feminine.

Waistline? Small.
Physique? Toned and lean.
Hips? Not too big.
Rear? Same.
Chest? Perky and large.
Wardrobe? Flattering and in fashion.
Style? Unique, but not *too* unique.
Bonus points for great shoes.

Those are the positives we see in our beauty-math. That is the beauty we seek.

Think of how destroyed you felt when a person made fun of some part of your appearance. Or think of how hopeless things seemed when you last compared your looks to that girl's from across the hall at school. You know, *that* girl. Or—think about how much money you spent the last time you went clothes shopping, or how much time you expend every day putting on makeup or styling your hair or working out, because you feel so much pressure to look *right*. Think about how you rushed to the nearest bathroom, mortified and desperately hunting for concealer, when you felt that latest zit coming on.

It's all so familiar, isn't it?

A certain kind of physical appearance equals beauty. You and I both know that our friends, our peers, and even we ourselves buy into this lie sometimes. Maybe we even buy into it a lot. We believe that looking a particular way is the true key to being beautiful. We chase after this standard for beauty, even though it is narrow and shallow. Even though it is judgmental and hurtful and impossible.

A certain kind of physical appearance—no. We couldn't be more wrong in believing all that.

A person could have every single physical feature on our world's beauty wish list—and still think she's a zero. She could fit our culture's definition of beautiful to a tee, yet feel worthless to the core. Underneath her supposedly attractive exterior, she could be dissatisfied, disappointed, insecure, lost, even desperate. In a word: empty.

It's no secret that having a model's appearance will open some doors in a young woman's life. I'm sure I don't have to point out that people who look a certain way are often rewarded with praise, attention, money, popularity, and all kinds of other things. But if we were to shine a light into the lives of these same young women, it wouldn't take long to find many who are absolutely miserable.

Yes, that girl who is so physically attractive and whose life is supposedly so fabulous as a result—maybe she feels cheap because people only ever notice her looks. Or she's sad, longing to be appreciated for something other than her outer shell. Or she gets desperate about maintaining her appearance, worried that if it fades, all the perks will go away too.

Not only that, but if you talk with enough young women, you'll see that anyone can look in the mirror and wish she saw something different there. No matter how pretty others say a woman is, in her own skin she might feel utterly unbeautiful. There's a simple explanation why: Physical appearance doesn't fill a person. It never will. It can't.

But there is something that can, does, and will forever. That something is real beauty.

Real beauty comes from the richest, fullest, most meaningful place that exists. It encompasses the most striking, appealing, and inviting qualities that could ever be.

It flows out of someone who—when we come to know and understand him for who he is—outshines anything else that we could ever think of as beautiful.

Real beauty is alive. It is life. There is nothing shallow about it, nothing temporary, nothing that can cause it to fade. Nothing—not disapproval from others, not the passage of time, not unwanted changes, not even a traumatic accident—can subtract from it. And everything about it is absolutely true.

Here is the truth:
God's love in your heart is your beauty.

God's love. It's as simple as that. This book is about how God's love makes a person breathtaking.

Every word and every sentence in these pages is here to show you how the Maker of all creation can remake you with his love. He does it by giving you the most remarkable gift in all of history, which is available to you this instant. Yes, all the fullness of beauty can be yours, right now.

How do you get it? As the chapters here will show, the process is less about you getting it and more about God giving it to you. It's a two-step deal, and both of the steps are directed by him.

First God gives you himself.
Then his love makes you more like himself.

He grips your heart, and he changes it. Each of these steps is marked with beauty: The fact that God gives you himself proves that he finds you beautiful. When his love begins to transform your heart, that beauty renews you from the inside out.

This process is not about you working hard to become

the kind of person God might accept. It's about God choosing to accept you, in spite of the ways you don't measure up to his standards. Through his Son, God does everything required to make you acceptable. More than acceptable: loved.

It's a jolt to the system, being pursued like this. The gift of God's love washes over you and makes you different. It puts God's imprint on your heart, so much that you begin to take on aspects of who he is. His love becomes alive in you: rich, abundant, and meaningful. Striking, appealing, inviting. It is undeniable beauty. It shines.

But how, really, does it happen?

When you dive into this book, you'll find that the chapters are divided into six sections. The first two sections (*Your Seeking Heart* and *Your Changed Heart*) focus on the first part of the beauty process: God giving himself to us. In these chapters, we'll look at why we need God, why we can trust him, how he gives himself to us, and what that means in general. The remaining four sections of the book look at specific areas of life where God's love transforms our hearts: through obedience (*Your Obedient Heart*), in our relationships (*Your Heart for Others*), in how we view ourselves (*Your Distinctive Heart*), and in how we approach the future (*Your Heart Looking Forward*).

Breaking things down a little further, in each of the chapters of this book you'll find

- **A story.** Every chapter begins with a personal story from my life or from the life of another young woman, told to illustrate either a common question young women have or a common problem young women face.[1]

---

[1] While the stories in this book are true, many names and some details have been changed to conceal identities. Any changes to detail have been kept as minimal as possible to best preserve the integrity of the story and its meaning.

- **A lesson from the Bible.** Our main focus in this book will always be the Bible and what it has to say, both about God and about us. That's far more important than anything I could ever tell you—so I hope that by connecting God's Word with stories from today, you'll see how relevant, important, and meaningful the Bible is to a young woman's everyday questions and concerns. I hope you'll see, more and more, how knowing God through his Word makes your heart beautiful!

- **A summary sentence.** These are here to keep the overall message of this book simple and easy to remember and share. When a specific chapter connects with your heart, write the sentence down and keep it where you'll see it on a regular basis. Or share your favorite summaries with your friends, whether in person, on social media, in an encouraging note, or in some other creative way. Help yourself remember what real beauty is about, and help others discover real beauty along with you.

- **Discussion starters.** These questions are designed to help you apply the principles you've just read about in each chapter. They're there to help you take the content of this book further, prodding you to think about specific ways that God wants to impact *your* heart and *your* life. Please don't skip the discussion starters! No chapter of this book is complete without them.

There's something about honest conversation that cements important ideas in us, and it's always great to have relationships where you can share what's on your heart, offering support and having a place to go when you need support. That's why the discussion starters at the end of each chapter are so important. This book will bring up ideas that you'll want cemented in your heart, and it will bring up ideas that might be tough to tackle. For that reason I recommend that you start a small group or grab a few friends who can read through this book with you, talking and praying together about what it's teaching you. It would be great if you had at least one mature Christian woman participating along with you to bring added experience and wisdom to your discussions. Grab your mom or your youth leader and ask her to read along. (Moms and youth leaders love invitations like that!)

As you read and discuss, take time especially to look at what God's Word can teach you and then let those truths sink in deeply. Pray about them. Learn from them. Work to obey them. Enjoy seeing them come alive in your life and in the lives of others—you'll never experience a more stunning ride.

Nothing can begin to compare with the love God gives. So come with me, won't you? Let's discover more and more what real beauty can be. Let's focus on how it can take hold of us and change us. Let's be awed by the One who makes it all possible.

And finally, let's choose to receive God's beauty and watch it overwhelm our hearts and radiate from within.

Part One

Your Seeking Heart

Your HEART is at the center of GOD'S HEART

A *Heart* at the Center

Warehouses and Wardrobe Closets: A *Gossip Girl* Story

There were no shiny hotels, mansions, or skyscrapers around—instead you saw only old warehouses, water towers, fire escapes, and a giant smokestack. The area looked more like a run-down shipping quarter than a luxurious backdrop for filming. But the set of *Gossip Girl* was located in this gritty New York City neighborhood.

For two months in my early twenties, I interned in the *Gossip Girl* wardrobe closet, and I can tell you that the show's closet was just as unfancy as the studio's location. It looked nothing like the fashion hub that people might've expected it to be. It looked like a dry-cleaning business.

Picture a big room with plain beige walls, a bare cement floor, and industrial fluorescent lights hanging from the ceiling. Racks of clothes were stacked two-high, with so many different pieces of clothing smashed onto them—any

and every pattern, style, texture, and color—that nothing seemed to match or coordinate at all. Boxes that held designer shoes were piled haphazardly. Signature gowns could go completely unnoticed. Most of the clothes you couldn't even see; everything seemed lost among endless wire hangers and cheap plastic garment bags.

There is a reason why none of this ever made it to the TV screen.

If you know anything about *Gossip Girl*, you probably know it told stories of a group of young socialites from New York City's (very wealthy, very fancy) Upper East Side. The characters on the show lived lives that were spilling over with posh parties, expensive fashion, jet-setting travel, and ritzy gifts. Week after week, lavishness and glamour played out on-screen.

So it shouldn't be surprising that bland warehouses and unassuming wardrobe closets weren't what people saw when they tuned in to *Gossip Girl*. Even though the warehouse and the wardrobe were important parts of what made the show work, they weren't what the show was about. The people who ran the show had decided what it was about, and that was Manhattan fantasy. Shimmering sets. Opulence. Fifth Avenue glam.

In making that decision, whether they realized it or not, the people in charge had also made another decision. That's because deciding what a show is about means also deciding what the show *isn't* about. If your story centers on New York glitz, then you're not going to be filming back lots and badly lit closets and streets in Queens. That's why the less-than-glamorous side of *Gossip Girl* never showed up on a TV screen. Most of it wasn't ever filmed at all.

This principle—the warehouses and wardrobe closets principle—is also true when we look at the Bible.

The Bible tells a story. It's one big story made up of lots of smaller stories, much like how a TV show is one big series made up of smaller episodes. All the stories in the Bible are about something. They're about the big story. In the next chapter, we're going to take a good look at what that big story is and what it means. Before we do that, though, we're going to take a good look at what the big story of the Bible *isn't*.

What it *doesn't* center on.

What it spends extremely little time mentioning.

These things that *aren't* the Bible's big story can often be clues for us, if we pay attention to them. That's because the Bible is the most important message ever. And the most important message ever wouldn't be missing something so vital. So if an issue gets barely any page space in the Bible, that's saying something about how unimportant the issue probably is.

We can take this logic one step further: If an issue almost never shows up in the Bible, yet in our lives we treat that issue as if it's supremely important, we're probably *really* missing the point of things.

For example, the Bible has almost nothing to say about physical appearance.

Looking into the Looks Void

If you're familiar with the Bible, think about some of the most well-known stories in it, and think of the people in the stories. What did those people look like?

- Abraham—was he tall or short?
- David—did he have freckles, or didn't he?

- Deborah—was her hair curly or straight or some kind of wavy in-between?
- Mary, Jesus' mother—were her eyes widely or narrowly set, almond-shaped or round, dark or light in color?

For us, any attempt to answer questions like these would be just a guess. We don't have the information because the details aren't included in the Bible anywhere. In fact, if we were to read the Bible from beginning to end, looking for specifics about people's physical attributes, we wouldn't find much.

Among the thousands of people mentioned in the Bible's pages, there's an extremely small number of them whose looks get any page space at all. We know limited details like: Esau was red and hairy, and his brother, Jacob, wasn't. Leah had dull eyes, and her sister Rachel was beautiful. Saul was tall. David was handsome. Eglon was overweight. Zacchaeus was short.

It's not a lot. But even when a few particulars about appearance *do* show up in the Bible, they're typically just tiny pieces in a story that's really about something else. Esau's hairiness is worth mentioning because when Jacob pretended to be Esau, he had to wear animal skins on his arms. Leah and Rachel's physical differences played into their competitive, jealous relationship. Saul's height made him a desirable king for Israel. David's handsomeness was just one more thing that made Saul hate him. Eglon's weight is mentioned in the story of his assassination—the dagger that killed him had sunk into his belly fat. Zacchaeus was too short to see Jesus over the crowds, so he climbed a tree to obtain a better view.

And even Jesus, the pivotal person in the whole Bible, is never described in terms of his appearance. The book of Isaiah includes a well-known prophecy that looks ahead to Jesus, mentioning a few details—

> *There was nothing beautiful or majestic about his appearance, nothing to attract us to him. . . .*
> *We turned our backs on him and looked the other way.*[1]

—but other than that, nothing. No hair color, no eye color, no height, no weight, no skin tone, no body mass, no facial structure. Zero. This is the Son of God, the turning point of the universe and certainly the Bible's main character, and we're not even given a basic mental picture.

From Genesis to Revelation, the Bible is essentially void of any commentary on looks. If we're paying attention to that, we learn something crucial. Because what a thing is *not* tells us a lot.

Let's put it this way: If you wanted to read about a new weight-lifting technique, you'd find a fitness magazine. If you wanted to figure out recipes and dinner ingredients, you'd get a cookbook. If you wanted to remodel your bathroom, you'd check out a home improvement show. If you wanted to landscape your yard, you'd visit a gardening blog. If you wanted to focus on your looks, you'd go to a salon. A boutique. A shoe store.

You wouldn't go to the Bible for any of these things because the Bible is barely concerned with them, if it's concerned about them at all.

How about we state the obvious for a moment? When God set out to write down his message for humanity, that message wasn't anything like *Dress for Your Body Type!* or *30 Days to Killer Abs!* or *Shape Your Brows Now!* For that matter, God's message wasn't *Grow the Best Begonias!* or *50 Vegan Appetizers!* or *Perfect Your Push-up!* either.

One of the most difficult and most amazing things about reading the Bible is that its message is drastically different from anything else we will ever encounter. Unlike our culture and unlike ourselves, the Bible doesn't waste time on shallow points or empty entertainment. It doesn't get caught up in distractions or fillers. What the Bible *does* is cut straight through to the center of everything. That's why God's Word includes what it includes, and that's why it doesn't include what it doesn't.

We can't read God's Word in the same way that we'd read a fashion magazine. We can't approach it in the same way that we'd approach a workout lesson. We shouldn't expect it to behave like a self-help book or a collection of wise thoughts to ponder either. We have to read it for what it is, not for what it isn't. And when we read God's Word for what it is, what we find is an epic love story.

Yes, *epic*. We should be blown away by what this book does to our hearts.

Read the Bible, and what you'll find—over and over, from Genesis to Revelation—is that your heart is at the center of God's heart. That is his message to you. Of everything he could've chosen to say, that is what he wanted you to know.

But wait. In case you're somehow not awestruck already, let me make sure I'm expressing the situation adequately:

> *The God who flung the stars into the sky*
> *and hand-formed every universe*
> *is obsessed with your heart.*

Yes, *obsessed*. That's what his Book is about, and it's a direct reflection of what he himself is about.

The God we meet in the Bible is consumed with the process that turns human hearts from being hardened and sinful to tender and beautiful. This God will do anything—in fact, he *has* done *everything*—to bring true beauty into your life and to make it radiate from the inside out.

Don't believe me? Keep reading.

> *A beautiful heart understands that*
> *God's focus isn't on looks.*

Discussion Starters

1. Look up 1 Samuel 16, especially verse 7. What is happening in this story? What does verse 7 tell us about God's perspective?

2. In what ways does our world center on looks? What should it tell us when our world's focus is so different from what we find in God's Word?

3. "God is obsessed with your heart." Do you believe this? Why or why not?

02

A *Heart* That Is Loved

**She Doesn't Believe God
Could Ever Love Her:
An Addiction Story**

*S*everal of my friends—a couple of them are close friends—struggle with addictions. Some are addicted to alcohol; some are addicted to painkillers; some are addicted to more than one harmful substance. But all of these friends have seen firsthand how addiction produces a ripple effect of big problems and big pain in life.

There's Shelby, for example. She's an alcoholic, and her addiction to drinking impacts nearly every corner of her life. In particular, it has a negative effect on her relationships, and then those relationships have a negative effect on the way Shelby views herself.

Here's one way that happens: Like everybody, Shelby has to make choices about her social plans. But when Shelby makes choices about how she'll spend her time, often at least one of the options she's considering is terrible: being in a place where there's alcohol in abundance, and hanging out with people who'll let her drink as much as she wants. (Often these people are drinking unhealthy amounts of alcohol too.)

Shelby could choose to spend time with friends who want the best for her, who would work to help her resist drinking. And she could choose to avoid places where alcohol flows freely. But the grip that drinking has on her is tight, so when she makes her plans, she often chooses the terrible option: the place that will let her drink a lot and the people who'll approve.

That's one way the ripple effect begins for Shelby, because people who are willing to watch a friend drink excessively are basically saying they don't care if that person treats her body like trash. They're encouraging her harmful habit, and they're doing nothing to help her stop. Some of them, in fact, seem to *like* that she's willing to treat her body in a destructive way. They seem to assume it gives them permission to do the same.

Too many of the men whom Shelby has met while drinking have treated her badly. Often they've used her in relationships that involve cheap pleasure but no real commitment. Once those guys are bored with her, they leave in a hurry. After they're gone, there's another ripple effect: Shelby feels ashamed, foolish, and cast aside. She blames herself for choosing the terrible option again. All along, she knows she shouldn't have even considered it.

Even when she's regretting her poor choices and trying to wish away rejection or mistreatment, Shelby drinks some more. But no matter how much liquid she pours down her throat, it won't do anything to make the pain go away. She knows it won't. It's just the same terrible decision one more time.

Ripple, ripple, ripple.

Still, Shelby's biggest problem isn't alcohol. In fact, in many ways Shelby's alcohol addiction is just a symptom of her ultimate problem. That ultimate problem is simple, but it has enormous ripples too: Shelby doesn't believe God could ever love her. When she looks at her life and some of the rotten, disastrous decisions she's made, she assumes her case is closed. Closed and doomed.

Shelby thinks it's possible to be beyond God's repair and long gone from his reach. She thinks her behavior is so bad that God could never look at her and respond with kindness or joy. She couldn't be more wrong.

No Cop on a Cross: The Forgiveness Story

Often we let ourselves think that God works like a police officer out on patrol. We tell ourselves he's scanning crowds and traffic lanes, watching and waiting for opportunities to punish our bad behavior. If we're good and obey his rules, he'll reward us by letting us go penalty-free. But if we're bad—if we disobey his rules, and especially if we know his rules and *still* disobey—he's going to blast us.

We assume God isn't sure yet how he'll respond to us. We assume our actions, good or bad, okay or terrible, are part of the equation that will eventually help him decide.

That's not how the Bible tells God's story, though. That doesn't even come close.

The central story of the Bible can be summarized like this:

> *God made a good world and put people in it, and he loved those people. This is obvious because he gave them everything they needed and everything they*

could have wanted, and the best thing he gave them was all of himself. He walked with them and talked with them and let them enjoy a seemingly endless supply of good things. There was only one part of creation, a single tree's fruit, that he told them they couldn't have.

But God's love and total abundance wasn't enough for the people. They didn't trust that God wanted the best for them and had already given them the best. They wondered if this forbidden fruit meant he was withholding from them. They believed Satan's lie that something other than God and his good gifts could make life better.

So they ate the fruit even though God, who loved them, had told them not to do it. And they found out right away that it didn't make life better. It brought shame and fear into their lives. It brought pain and brokenness into their relationships. It brought death.

This is not what God wanted for his people. But by the time God's people figured out that they should've trusted his love all along, they had already defied his love completely. Their mistrust couldn't be undone.

Or could it?

By the time God's people realized that his love actually was real and full and true, it was too late.

Or was it?

God loved his people more than words can say, even after they had made a joke of his love.

And although they deserved the terrible things that their sin had earned, God still wanted the best for them instead. He wanted them to have all of himself again, forever. He wanted to help them trust him so they could know how incredible it is to love fully, like he does.

So he set out, right then and there, to make an everlasting fix for people's untrusting, dying hearts. He knew they could never repair their hearts on their own, so he took the weight upon himself.

God sent part of himself—his Son, Jesus Christ—into the now broken world. Jesus is God in human form, which means that even though he lives in a body, he has the exact same character and mind as God, his Father. Because of that, Jesus could be the link between God and people.

God knew that Jesus could live in the world like people do, and God knew that, unlike people, Jesus could live in the world and still trust God's love completely. Jesus could respond to God's love perfectly too, by obeying his Father with joy and by loving him fully.

During his time on earth, Jesus did all this. He did it just like God knew he would. And because Jesus did, he earned the best reward, the one that God had longed to give all people from the beginning: eternal life with God, enjoying God's love.

Now here is the most incredible part of this story: After Jesus had rightfully earned his eternal life, God didn't reward him with it. Instead, God punished him with the worst kind of death: torture and crucifixion. This was not a surprise to Jesus— remember, he has God's exact character and mind. He chose terrible death for himself.

As Jesus died, God turned his back on his Son. This was the unthinkable part. Their love, which had always been perfect and fully united, was utterly betrayed and broken. It was the ultimate punish- ment, the one that God's sinful people had been earning since centuries before, when they first began defying his love.

But God refused to turn his back on people. He loved them too much. Instead, he saved total punishment and betrayal only for himself. He made the biggest swap ever: By dying the death that people's sin had earned, God (through Jesus) made it possible for people to be off the hook for their own punishment. And then, as an illustration of God's mighty power and his triumph even over death, Jesus rose again! He's alive today! With the death penalty taken away, God could offer people the gift he had longed to give them since the first day he created them: eternal life—all of himself and all of his love, without end! He wanted people to have this gift so badly that he was willing to die to make it possible.

That's how much God loved his people. That's how much he loves you. That's how strong his love is: stronger than all sin and sinfulness, no matter how terrible and hopeless it may seem.

"It is finished!" Those were the last words Jesus spoke on the cross before he died.[2] I love reading those words. "It is finished" helps me remember that God's love isn't a response based on whether I obey or disobey him. God is not in the process of evaluating sins to figure out whether or not he can love and forgive a person. He made that decision long ago, for you and me and Shelby and everyone else too.

God loves people so much that he wants to give us the good standing we don't deserve. He wants to give his forgiveness and Jesus' righteousness. He doesn't require us to earn it by being perfect or good or even mostly obedient. He knows we could never manage that. Our sinful hearts would block the way constantly.

And God knows how sinful our hearts are. He knows they are unspeakably dark and terrible sometimes. How could he not know that? The evilness of sin is why it took something as huge as Jesus' death to pay sin's price. God even knew that some people would not accept his amazing, free gift of forgiveness and righteousness, even after Jesus' death had bought it.[3] Still, God was glad to settle the price of sin, once and for all.

If you're wondering whether or not God could love you, there's no reason to wonder. He can. He does. He has. His love for you has been true for all eternity. It has already gone as far as love can possibly go. Nothing you do can cancel his love or force it away.

It is finished. You are loved more than you could ever dream.

*A beautiful heart knows that it's impossible to
be beyond God's repair or out of his reach.*

Discussion Starters

1. The message that Jesus died in our place and freely gives us his righteousness is known as the *gospel*, which means "good news." Why is the word *gospel* and its meaning so fitting?

2. Have you ever thought that God is like a cop on patrol? How does the story of his love change that?

3. How does it impact you, knowing that God loves you as much as he does?

03

A *Heart* That Receives

Couple Patrol: A School Dance Story

$\mathscr{P}$atrick, the first guy I ever *really* liked, had invited me to his high school dance, and I was thrilled.

Each of us dressed up, we took some pictures, and then we drove together to a beautiful private ranch in the Dallas area. It was the home of one of the girls from Patrick's school, and she and her family were hosting and chaperoning the dance there. They had decked out the whole place with special lighting and decorations, hired a great DJ, and brought in all kinds of tasty food and drinks.

I knew almost all the other students at the dance. Even though I didn't go to class with them, their school was owned and operated by the church my family belonged to at the time. Nearly all these students were part of that church too, and some of them were my closest friends. We loved spending time together, and most of us were

enjoying the fancy night out, dancing, eating, talking, and laughing.

Most of us.

Out on the dance floor, one person was so busy performing couple-patrol that I'm not sure he enjoyed himself at all. That person was Neil, another student and one of Patrick's friends. Neil seemed to have appointed himself the one to make sure none of the dancing got out of hand. Patrick and I discovered this in the middle of a slow dance when Neil stopped us abruptly and awkwardly.

"Leave some room for Jesus," he said.

Now, I know that during slow songs at school dances, couples can sometimes get embarrassingly close and too physically familiar. I also know that this was *not* one of those times. Patrick and I were dancing, sure, but we hadn't mashed our bodies together or anything like that. At most, what was happening between us was a light hug and some swaying back and forth to music.

Still, Neil did not approve. It was clear he thought we shouldn't approve either. He stood there waiting, until Patrick and I moved far enough apart that Jesus could apparently fit between us. Then, satisfied, Neil left. Later, I saw him repeat the same spacing process with two of my friends.

Had I heard the phrase "Leave some room for Jesus" that night from anyone except Neil, it would've sounded like a joke. But Neil had a way of getting worked up about what people might be doing, whether it was something clearly wrong or whether it had even a small possibility of turning wrong.

Neil was aghast when he found out that a high schooler he knew had smoked a cigarette. He frequently scolded his friends for any behavior that might potentially be out of line by asking, "Now, is that honoring to Christ?" He made himself the behavior police wherever he went, and he never seemed to be off duty.

You Can't Earn Free Forgiveness

We talked in chapter 2 about one kind of person who needs the gospel. We looked at my friend Shelby, whose addiction to alcohol keeps her from believing that God could look past her sin. The good news of the gospel emphasizes to a person like Shelby that there's no sin so big or so awful that it could ever get in the way of God's enormous love.

But there's another kind of person who needs the gospel's amazing news too. This person is probably not an alcoholic; in fact, she's more likely to be one of the most self-controlled churchgoers you know, one of the "goodiest" good girls you could find in a youth group. Or maybe, like Neil, this person is the sort of guy who's paranoid about any hint of disobedience, who might stand guard on school dance floors to make sure no one goes too far during a slow song.

There are important truths about God that this person has trouble believing too. Often their relentlessly obedient behavior is proof.

Let's remember: God interacts with us in a way that's different from anything we're used to seeing in our human relationships. God offers forgiveness to us freely. The cost of it has been fully paid for by Jesus' death. Anything we could ever owe God because of our sin is, because of Jesus, covered. There is no remaining balance on our account. That's what "freely" means.

In Romans 11, the Bible explains it this way:

God's grace [is] his undeserved kindness in choosing [us].
And since it is through God's kindness, then it is not by
[our] good works. For in that case, God's grace would not
be what it really is—free and undeserved.[4]

When God saves us and offers us eternal life with him, it's a gift, through and through. It has already been purchased—no part of it still needs to be bought or earned—and God is handing it to us eagerly. The only thing left for us to do is receive it. Receiving is the only piece that any of us can contribute to God's forgiveness puzzle.

Forgiveness, like any other gift, has an effect on us. Typically the receiver has a positive response to the giver. For example, if someone gives you a birthday gift, you want to thank them, and you probably feel a little more devotion to them. The gift has sweetened the relationship.

In the same way, when God offers us his forgiveness, it makes sense that we would respond to that gift with thankfulness and with heartfelt commitment to God. Usually this will look like joy and obedience. (We'll talk more specifically about these later.) So there's nothing unbiblical about a forgiven person wanting to obey God and please him. Further, there's nothing strange about a forgiven person wanting to obey and please God *a lot*. That's how it should be, in fact. Joyful obedience is a natural effect of having received so much. Obedience is energized directly by God's incredible gift.

There *is* something strange—something unbiblical, in fact—about a person wanting to obey God and please him, when that person's main focus is their own obedience rather than God's free gift. Obeying for the sake of obedience means you feel pressure to obey. It means you

think your ability to obey is more important to the puzzle than God's ability to completely forgive you. Obeying for the sake of obedience means there's a part of your heart that doesn't fully believe in God's free forgiveness. Instead, you're trying to earn it. You're trying to prove, with all kinds of good behavior and rule following, that you can deserve God and that he should accept you.

But he already accepts you. He knows you'll never manage to get rid of your sinfulness. He knows your heart is sinful, and he loves you anyway. He lived the only sinless life and the only truly good life on your behalf, because he knew you couldn't do it. He put every ounce of pressure on himself. It's silly to try to pick up some of it for yourself when he has already carried it all.

You can come to God freely, without trying to get better or improve yourself first. He will give you rest and joy, knowing that *you*—not your goodness or your efforts or your obedience—are perfectly enough already. You're perfect in his eyes, not because of anything you've done or could do, but because he has been perfect for you.

A beautiful heart sees that God gives
love and forgiveness freely—
it's impossible to earn them.

Discussion Starters

1. What does it mean that God's grace is free? What does that tell you about how much God loves people?

2. "He put every ounce of pressure on himself. It's silly to try to pick up some of it for yourself when he has already carried it all." Do you think of God's forgiveness in this way? Explain.

3. What can you do to keep your obedience thankful and focused joyfully on God's grace?

04

A *Heart* That Believes

When My Parents Were Divorced: A Prayer Story

A sheriff's officer knocked on our front door one evening around bedtime when my twin sister, Brittany, and I were four. It was an official visit, and it came as a complete shock to everyone in the house except my mom. The officer was there to serve my dad with divorce papers.

My parents had been married for nine years. They had worked hard to build our family's life, and it was a life that probably seemed great from the outside looking in. But neither of my parents was walking closely with God back then, and their hearts needed him. Their relationship showed it.

My mom had been having an affair with another man for about a month by the time she initiated the split with my dad. She had already told my dad that she didn't love him anymore and that maybe she had never loved him. But

she hadn't *really* been honest with him—she didn't know how to be. She also didn't have a practice of turning to God for comfort in the times her marriage felt lonely. Instead she ended up talking with someone else, finding comfort from that man, and eventually turning to him. Even though she felt guilty about it, she was letting her heart be stolen by someone other than her husband.

On my dad's side, he had seen for a while that my mom was struggling, and he had heard her try to express that to him. He had even begged her to go to marital counseling with him. He seemed willing to do anything to make their relationship right again and to salvage what they once had. But none of that kept my mom from walking away completely, and when she left him, my dad didn't have the fullness of faith to help him get through. What he had instead was emptiness, enormous anger, and deep heartbreak.

Over the next few years, though, both my mom and my dad got involved in churches. They each started reading the Bible regularly and studying God's character. Little by little, they were learning. As a result, they were changing. Six months after their divorce was final, my mom made a renewed commitment to God, accepting his love and forgiveness and trusting him with her life. At that same time, she made sure that Brittany and I had our own Bibles—she wanted us to know God and his love for us too.

Brittany and I became Christians at the age of seven. By that time, believing in God and following him made simple sense to each of us. We were young, but we had already learned a lot about God in church and from our parents, and we trusted that what we had been told about God was true. We even believed he could do miracles.

God could do miracles—what a perfect thing! Brittany and I felt we needed a miracle, and we wanted one more than anything. If God could create the universe, bring dead people back to life, and turn water into the best wine, then certainly he could bring our parents back together. Couldn't he?

As much as we were hoping it could happen, we also knew the idea was a long shot. Our parents always treated each other kindly and politely, sure, but divorce is divorce— it doesn't happen unless at least one person *really* means it. When our mom left our dad, she had *really* meant it, and in the process, she had hurt him deeply. Even though God had turned both of their hearts toward him in the years that followed, nothing had changed about the status of their divorce papers.

Still, God could do miracles. Miracles!

Every night before bed, Brittany and I prayed that God would make what seemed impossible, possible. We asked God to miraculously transform our family and put it back in one piece. For years, we prayed that prayer. We waited and we believed.

My sister and I were children when we put our trust in God. Looking back on that time now, in some ways our faith seemed simplistic and naive. In some ways it was. But in important ways, it also wasn't.

Back then we believed that God is who he says he is and that his Word is true. We believed he cares about the things that concern us. We believed we should reach out for him when things turn dark. The older I get and the more I see God at work, the more I understand that we were absolutely right to believe all of this. And the more I understand why.

Is God Really Good?

If you do a little looking, you can see glimpses of God's loving faithfulness all around. Plenty of people have stories about how God healed them from an illness, provided something specific the moment they needed it, or mended a relationship in some beautiful way.

But those aren't *all* the stories. Sometimes you'll hear from people who've prayed and prayed without noticing any changes. They're still stuck in their painful relationships, still terribly in need, still sick or dying. Sometimes people in these circumstances question God or turn away from him as a result. They assume he doesn't care about them, that he couldn't possibly want them to have what's best.

When God doesn't do what we've asked him to do, it can be easy to lose ourselves in a harsh cycle of wondering why. We can become skeptical of God, doubting his character. But that's an example of piling on so many questions that the Answer gets covered up completely.

The day Jesus died on the cross, there were two criminals on crosses beside him. By the end of the day, both those criminals would be dead. One of the criminals was focused on those circumstances: He didn't want to die. He figured that if Jesus wouldn't change things by getting them all off their crosses alive, then Jesus couldn't be God. "So you're the Messiah, are you?" he said. "Prove it. . . ."[5]

But the other criminal believed. He wasn't focused on his circumstances; instead, he was looking at Jesus. He saw Jesus for who he was, trusting that God's Son had done no wrong. This criminal didn't waste final moments asking God to change earthly circumstances, not even when those circumstances involved his own execution.

Instead, he asked for the one thing that meant everything, especially in the face of death: "Jesus, remember me when you come into your Kingdom."

"I assure you," Jesus told him, "today you will be with me in paradise."[6]

Nothing that God could give us on earth compares with the gift of eternity with him. There is no greater example of goodness or generosity. It's not possible to be more loving than God has already been to us, allowing his Son to be murdered so that we could experience his love forever. Nothing else he could ever add would make that gift better.

God is good. If he had any whisper of selfishness or cruelty in him, he wouldn't have died for us. He would have let us receive death and hell like we deserve. But instead he took on the brutal pain of our sin so we could have eternal life with him.

We can't make sense of God by looking at our circumstances. We make sense of our circumstances by looking at God. He loves us. No matter what comes our way, we can trust that he is good, that his Word will guide us tenderly, and that his care will comfort us when things seem at their worst.

God wants what's best for us, and often what's best for us is *way* off our own radar. God knows that sometimes it's best for us to learn patience, waiting on him and praying faithfully, maybe for years on end. He knows that sometimes we can't see the whole picture and that what we're asking him for right now is not actually as promising as it may seem. He knows that sometimes the most heartbreaking experiences are what cause us to seek after him with total hunger and that pain can actually be the quickest road to sheer joy.

And he knows that sometimes—not always and not even usually, but sometimes—another miracle is just what this doubting world needs to help it believe.

After seven years of divorce, my parents remarried. Just after we'd finished fifth grade, they picked up Brittany and me from summer camp one day and told us the astonishing news. God had healed each of their hearts toward the other. His love had made both of them new, and he had given them confidence that their relationship could be made new too.

It has been. My parents' second marriage is almost fifteen years old now, and in significant ways it is different from their first. God has taught my mom that she can be honest with my dad, trusting that my dad will do his best to love her selflessly, like God has loved him. And God has taught my dad that he should notice my mom's concerns and work to care for them, knowing that that's how God cares for us.

Still, my parents' remarriage isn't the best part of this story. Their second wedding happened because a bigger thing had happened first. My mom and dad found God's love, and that's how they could find each other again. Knowing that God had given his life selflessly for them, they could learn ways to be selfless in relationships too.

They understood their circumstances differently when they understood that the most powerful being in the universe gave his love for them. Their perspective changed once they saw that his love is the best possible miracle.

A beautiful heart believes, no matter the circumstances, that God wants the best for people.

Discussion Starters

1. One criminal on a cross beside Jesus was promised
   paradise. What was that criminal's perspective of
   Jesus? What was the other criminal looking at?

2. "We make sense of our circumstances by looking
   at God." What does this mean?

3. What is difficult in your life right now? How can you
   remember God's goodness and trust him in spite of
   difficult circumstances?

· come let us ·

Worship

AND BOW DOWN.

let us kneel

BEFORE THE LORD

our maker

FOR HE IS

our God

· psalm 95:6-7 ·

05

A *Heart* That Worships

Too Good to Be True: A Kissing Story

My friend Lisa has been a Christian for as long as she can remember. For a long time, that meant Lisa's faith centered on being a "good" Christian.

As a teenager, Lisa wore modest clothes. She didn't curse. She didn't smoke, drink alcohol, or do drugs. At one point in middle school, she left her group of friends because they had begun following bad influences. On her high school cheerleading team, she protested against provocative movements in routines. These were all prices she seemed easily willing to pay. As a Christian, staying good was important.

Staying good was also why Lisa stayed "never been kissed" for a long time. She wanted to obey God's design and save sex for marriage, and she figured it would be a lot easier to do that if she didn't kiss anybody. So she made

a vow to God that she wouldn't kiss a guy until she got engaged. She even wrote a book and gave speeches about her commitment.[7]

Lisa was serious about honoring and obeying God, and she probably seemed more serious about it than most other people she knew. But what Lisa couldn't see was that she was setting herself up for a giant fall. Her goodness was too good to be true, because nobody is as honoring or as obedient to God as Lisa thought she needed to be.

One night in her midtwenties, after a lighthearted day at a wedding, Lisa found herself staying up late in a house with some bridesmaids and groomsmen. She was talking with Tom, a guy she had known for less than forty-eight hours. Then suddenly the two of them were alone. He put his arm around her—he was the first guy who had ever done that. It made her worry because he had no idea she had promised God that kissing was off the table.

Not wanting to break her vow, Lisa debated making a speech to Tom, right there on the couch. But that seemed more and more ridiculous, especially because she didn't want him to know she had kissing on the brain. So she didn't.

The thoughts in her head spun like crazy, until finally he kissed her. And she kissed him. Even worse, she partly liked it and kissed him again.

That's when her mind *really* reeled.

What in the world was she doing?!? Here she was, *not* engaged and *not* committed to a guy, tossing aside her vow almost effortlessly. And not just any vow. This was The Big Vow she had made. To God. As part of her faith. Breaking this particular vow felt like breaking something that belonged to God. It felt like breaking a vital part of her faith.

Lisa would tell you that it took a long time for her to get a solid grip on things again after that day. She didn't understand how to steer her Christian life anymore. For her, a history of stellar obedience had always been central to the deal, and now it wasn't. She had to admit she wasn't the pristine follower of God she had thought she was. That shook her.

So she prayed, a lot. On the advice of a trusted mentor, she read the book of Romans a lot too. Those two things eventually led her to a discovery that was startling. She realized that her vow and the whole business with Tom hadn't actually been about obedience after all. Even her obedience hadn't been about obedience.

All of it was about worship. Lisa had been busy worshiping the wrong thing when she needed to worship the right One instead.

Broken Tablets and Promises

> *All the people answered with one voice, "We will do everything the LORD has commanded."*[8]

The Israelites make this pledge just after God has miraculously rescued them out of slavery in Egypt. Now they're camping in a wilderness near Mount Sinai—but this is no ordinary camping trip. The Israelites are making a covenant (a legally binding agreement) with God. After Moses reads aloud the instructions the Lord has given him, the people unanimously promise to follow God alone.

A covenant is a big deal. It is about as far from an empty promise as you can get. In this time and place, it wasn't uncommon that if you broke your end of a covenant, your penalty would be death.

Because covenants are so serious, we can safely guess that the Israelites mean what they say when they tell God they will follow his commands. And why wouldn't they mean it? He has just proven that he is the loving God he said he is, swooping them up out of Egypt and slavery, and pointing them in the direction of abundance. He has just told them that he will love them exclusively, making them his special people for all time. All they need to do in return is obey.

God has a whole list of commandments for them to obey. Hundreds. And the commandment that kicks off the whole bunch is, "You must not have any other god but me."[9] This is significant.

The last step of the covenant-making process is that God calls the Israelites' representative and leader, Moses, up onto Mount Sinai to receive stone tablets. God has etched his laws for the people on the tablets. They're copies of the covenant, similar to what a signed legal document would be today. Both parties had agreed to the terms, so now it was official.

After Moses receives the stone tablets from God, he stays on Mount Sinai for forty days, finalizing Israel's promise to obey. The Israelites can see that something big is happening up there, because God has settled his presence on the mountain in the form of a powerful storm. Unfortunately, though, forty days is more time than it takes for the Israelites to not only rethink their side of the covenant but also to break it. By the time Moses reappears at the base of the mountain, God's people have made a calf-shaped golden idol and are already worshiping it.

Seeing this, Moses sends the stone tablets crashing

to the ground, shattering them. It's a symbol of the shattered covenant.

Now, it would seem easy at first to give the Israelites a hard time about this. But let's hold off on that for a moment. If we'll look closely at them while also looking honestly at ourselves, we'll have no problem seeing how we could've ended up in the same place.

Think about it. Was there ever a group of people that had better reasons to obey? Israel is on the heels of not just one but many miracles. God has parted the Red Sea and destroyed the Egyptian army so their slavery will end. He has sent plagues, making the Egyptians so miserable that they beg the Israelites to leave, shoving riches into their hands as they go. This means God's people have their freedom, God's promise to treasure them forever, *and* wealth to help them thrive. Plus they have a freshly minted covenant to help keep them in line.

If people under *these* circumstances can so easily put an idol in God's place, that's saying something about people. It's saying something about not only them but us, too.

Unfortunately, like the ancient Israelites, we have a way of losing sight of God, even when he is thundering all around us. Like them, we easily forget his faithfulness to us and our promises to him. Like them, it doesn't take much for us to put idols in God's place.

You might think, *Really—idols?* Yes. Although we don't make calf-shaped golden idols these days, we do make them. We set them up in our hearts, and we worship them just the same.

A great definition of modern-day idolatry comes from a pastor out of New York City. He says that we make an idol in our heart when we make anything except God our ultimate thing. An idol, he says, is the thing that, if you lost it, would make your world fall apart.[10]

There's only one thing—and it's not a thing, it's a being—that, if we lost it, would actually cause our world to fall apart. God is that being. Anything else we can live without. So when we accept in our hearts that there's something *other than God* that we must have to survive, it means we're giving that something the kind of credit that only God deserves. We're putting that thing in God's place, which is another way of saying that we're worshiping it. We're making it an idol.

We can make idols out of all kinds of things, and they don't always seem harmful at first glance. Take Lisa and her no-kissing vow, for instance. While it might've seemed like Lisa was serving God, we can see that she wasn't. We can see this because when Lisa's obedience fell apart, her world fell apart. Her idol was "being obedient to God," which is a fabulous thing—unless it's your ultimate thing.

Each of us has our own idol or idols we're tempted to worship in God's place. Some examples of the idols we serve are friendship, success, approval, romance, status, security, blending in, standing out, getting stuff, having health, building a stellar reputation, living conflict-free, or looking a certain way. If you don't know what your idol is, you'll likely find a clear picture emerging if you answer questions like these:

- What/whom do you take the most risks for?
- What/whom do you give the most time to?
- What/whom do you spend the most money on?
- What/whom do you make the most excuses for?

- What/whom do you talk about most?
- What/whom do you think about most?
- What/whom are you most defensive about?

Now, assuming you have an idol in mind, here's the incredible news about it: It is no more threatening to God than the ancient Israelites' golden calf was. The worship of that calf angered God intensely (and it should have!) because the Israelites were being unfaithful to him. Still, ultimately he was faithful in his promises to them even though they had so easily broken theirs to him.

God made them his treasure. He gave up everything for their good. He created a way, through Jesus, that he could look at them and be completely satisfied. Unlike with an idol, which always wants more, with God, there was nothing more that needed to be done.

That is who God was, and it is also who God *is*. He makes *us* his treasure. He gave up everything for *our* good. He created a way, through Jesus, that he could look at *us* and be completely satisfied. The doing is done.

What an amazing love! What a source of joy! What a reason to worship! Even though we are unfaithful, his promises remain. Which is why, in the end, knowing him crushes the allure of every idol that seeks to attract our attention.

> Come, let us worship and bow down.
>   Let us kneel before the LORD our maker,
>   for he is our God.
> We are the people he watches over,
>   the flock under his care.

PSALM 95:6-7

A beautiful heart worships God,
ordering life around him alone.

Discussion Starters

1. "If people under *these* circumstances can so easily put an idol in God's place, that's saying something about people. It's saying something about . . . us, too." What about the Israelites' circumstances should have made their commitment to God particularly strong?

2. "An idol . . . is the thing that, if you lost it, would make your world fall apart." What idol or idols are you most attracted to? What attracts you to it/them?

3. How have you seen, either in your own life or in someone else's, that idols are never satisfied? By contrast, where do we see that God's love is satisfied?

Part Two

Your Changed Heart

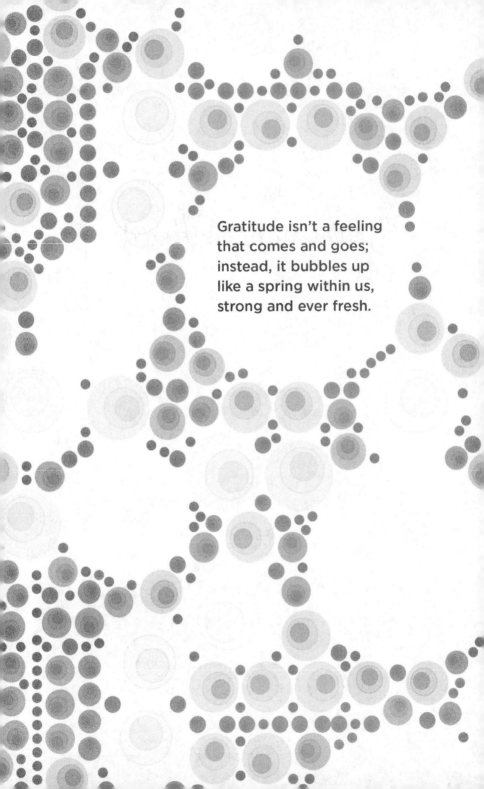

Gratitude isn't a feeling
that comes and goes;
instead, it bubbles up
like a spring within us,
strong and ever fresh.

06

A *Heart* That Says Thanks

Miss Mayola's Blessing: An Answered-Prayer Story

It wasn't out of the norm for Brittany and me to drop in on Miss Mayola. We met her through an inner-city ministry when we were younger, and over the years she had become like our Texas grandmother. We had been visiting her regularly for a long time. But on this day, even though it seemed just like any other, Miss Mayola thought our visit was extraordinary.

"You're my blessing! You're my blessing!" she kept exclaiming, with a big smile on her face.

It's a simple story from a simple day, but it became a remarkable moment for Brittany and me. It's the kind of simplicity that should be remembered.

Miss Mayola is a slightly slumped, five-foot-tall, ninety-two-year-old woman who lives in a run-down part of South Dallas. She's always wearing a nightgown—a white cotton one, usually with a small, sweet print. The white calls extra attention to her eyes and her big smile, and it helps bring out the richness in her deep brown, wrinkly skin and her thick and wiry gray hair. Miss Mayola's appearance is a plain kind of richness. That's how her whole life is, really.

The area where her little white house stands is not the sort of place that Dallas likes to be known for. It has run-down homes, boarded-up buildings, and a consistent dose of crime. The neighborhoods can be very unsafe. Still, this is where Miss Mayola has spent her entire life, and she's comfortable in it. Her home even has flowers out front—some church members planted them for her a while ago.

Inside the house, it's always hot. That's how Dallas is without air-conditioning, and Miss Mayola doesn't have money to cool things down. She also can't afford new furniture—what she has is tattered and a little grungy, with years of spills and sweat built up in the fabric. Then there's garbage on top of that. There's garbage on top of pretty much everything at Miss Mayola's. Maybe it's because she owns so little that she likes to keep what she has, even if it has become dirty or useless.

This little home is where she spends nearly all her time. It's where she sleeps, eats, greets guests, gives hugs, and prays. And believe me, Miss Mayola *prays*.

Every time she talks to God, she starts out the same way: "Our gracious Father who art in heaven, it is again your humble servant coming to you in the lowest manner I know how." Her voice is raspy and slightly high-pitched. When Miss Mayola is having a regular conversation, sometimes it can be difficult to understand what she is saying.

But not when she prays. When she prays, her words are as clear as anything.

The day Brittany and I visited, the day Miss Mayola thought the visit was exceptional, she had prayed a particular prayer before we arrived. She told us she had asked God for a blessing.

Now, there are plenty of blessings that our Texas grandmother could have asked God to give her. She could have asked for extra energy in her tired, old body, or a new, clean couch, or affordable air-conditioning, or a replacement nightgown, or some extra money for groceries, or some extra money for pretty much anything. There's a lot she could use in life that she doesn't have. But when she talked with God that day, she hadn't been specific. She had prayed for a blessing, then she had waited. What wonderful surprise would answer her prayer?

"You're my blessing!" she told us. She was absolutely thrilled. For her, our visit had solved the day's puzzle and answered an exhilarating riddle. Brittany and I were the good thing that God had decided to bring to her that day. She was sure of it.

"It's *you*!" Miss Mayola exclaimed. She clapped her hands excitedly and beamed from ear to ear, standing there in her worn nightie, in her small and shabby home, in her dangerous neighborhood, in the heat, in significant need. I'm not sure I've ever glimpsed a moment in which someone was more grateful.

Gratitude on Top of Gratitude

It's possible for gratitude to be simply a one-time response to something. People give us a gift or are especially kind in some circumstance, and their thoughtfulness in that moment makes us thankful. Most of the time, that's how we think about and "do" gratitude. When some time passes after the most recent kindness, we forget about it, and we stop feeling grateful until the next nice thing happens.

But there is a greater gratitude. This gratitude isn't a feeling that comes and goes based on what happens (or doesn't happen) to us day by day or minute by minute. Instead, it bubbles up like a spring within us, strong and ever fresh. This is the kind of gratitude people like Miss Mayola put on display. Their thankfulness doesn't depend on having extra attention, getting bonus presents, or being on the receiving end of service. This gratitude comes from a greater place.

We see a glimpse of this kind of gratitude in Mark 2, when Jesus heals a man who was paralyzed. This dramatic story has a lot to teach us about being thankful, in particular because the thankfulness it emphasizes has almost nothing to do with someone walking away on a set of healed legs.

The story goes like this: Early in Jesus' ministry, he was quickly getting a reputation for having healed lots of people. Because of this, when he came to one town, Capernaum, four men carried their paralyzed friend on a mat to where Jesus was. But the crowds around Jesus were too dense for the group of five to get through. So the mat-carriers climbed on top of the house, cut a hole in the roof, and lowered their friend into the room where Jesus was.

Jesus saw the faith of these men, so he looked at the paralyzed man and said, "My child, your sins are forgiven."[11]

Those of us who live in modern times and have been able to read the whole Bible have an unfair advantage

when reading stories like these. We tend to forget that in Jesus' day, plenty of people thought Jesus wasn't anything too special. Back then, there were many other rabbis who taught and had followers like Jesus did. In fact, because people didn't think Jesus was special, many of the things Jesus said made them furious. What he said to the paralyzed man is a perfect example.

Some of the men who taught religious laws heard Jesus speak and instantly thought he was cursing God. They didn't believe Jesus was God, and they knew that by claiming to forgive sins, he was putting himself on God's level. That, in their minds, was the worst kind of curse.

But Jesus knew these men's thoughts, so he kept going.

> *"Why do you question this in your hearts? Is it easier to say to the paralyzed man 'Your sins are forgiven,' or 'Stand up, pick up your mat, and walk'? So I will prove to you that the Son of Man has the authority on earth to forgive sins." Then Jesus turned to the paralyzed man and said, "Stand up, pick up your mat, and go home!"*
>
> *And the man jumped up, grabbed his mat, and walked out through the stunned onlookers. They were all amazed and praised God, exclaiming, "We've never seen anything like this before!"*[12]

It's an amazing story, right? But let's focus in on one detail here: Do you see whose praise this story *doesn't* talk about?

It doesn't talk about the healed man's praise. That doesn't mean it wasn't there—we can all safely assume it was—but that man's praise doesn't seem to be the point. Instead, the praise that's mentioned is the praise of everyone else. We should notice that, because there's something significant in it.

If the book of Mark had focused on the healed man's praise, it would be easier for us to focus on the healed man too. But the story here isn't about the healed man, at least not in the way we might initially think. Let's remember that the first thing Jesus gave that man wasn't the ability to walk. Jesus gave him the reason to believe: "Your sins are forgiven."

The reason why Jesus healed the man's legs was less about getting that man to walk and more about giving the onlookers a reason to believe too: "I will prove to you that the Son of Man has the authority on earth to forgive sins," Jesus told them. He wasn't healing this man to say, "Here's a nice change for a person," or "I can make broken bodies unbroken." He was saying, "Everyone! I have the power to forgive you!"

That's why the crowd became full of praise. The man's healing was a sign that everyone else watching could be healed, too, at the heart level. God's people had been waiting for their savior to arrive, the one who would be able to restore their hearts to God. Jesus was that Savior!

What we see here is that although Jesus gives many good gifts, one gift he gives outshines all the others. Even something miraculous like giving a paralyzed man instant stability on his feet doesn't hold a candle to God's gift of salvation and eternal grace. Unlike other gifts, God's for-*give*-ness is everlasting. It never fades. And because forgiveness never fades, the gratitude that stems from forgiveness can be constant too. Yes, *constant*. We can be grateful at every moment, because God gives the best gift, which doesn't ever go away.

That's the kind of gratitude Miss Mayola has. That's why she can be thankful even when life isn't perfectly comfortable and supplied for. Her heart has what it needs forever, and because of that, she knows she always has the ultimate reason to say, "Thank you."

And that's why, when a tiny blessing comes her way in the form of two visiting friends, she recognizes it as a blessing. She doesn't wonder where the other blessings are or question why God didn't give her something else instead; she's simply thankful. In fact, she *expects* to be thankful—she waits eagerly to see how God will bless her, trusting that he does and that he will.

When the simple visit comes, Miss Mayola receives it with massive praise. Not only has she received the best gift ever, now she has a bonus gift too! Every new blessing simply adds to her abundance, and in her heart, she has gratitude on top of gratitude.

A beautiful heart can be grateful at every moment, because God gives the best gift, which doesn't ever go away.

Discussion Starters

1. Do you ever focus on what you *don't* have instead of being grateful for what you *do* have? If so, how can remembering God's forgiveness change your heart?

2. Is God's forgiveness a constant source of life and strength for gratitude in your heart? If not, what do

you think that might suggest about how you view God's forgiveness?

3. What blessings in your life have you failed to recognize as blessings? What has God given you today and this week and this year that you haven't yet praised him for?

07

A *Heart* That Knows

The Bitter Soul Complains:
A Listening Story

For a while after my accident, I got intensely angry about pretty much everything.

I was really frustrated with the new changes I faced. Between physical therapy, counseling sessions, prostheses, medical bills, and checkups, my routine had changed drastically. My relationships had changed too. And the pain was just so terrible. It was so bad that sometimes huge doses of medication wouldn't make it go away.

While I believed that this must be God's plan for my life—this was what was happening, after all—I wasn't sure I wanted much to do with God's plan, if it was going to be like this.

There are plenty of people who wonder what you should say to God when you're mad, maybe even furious. When it feels like you've lost big parts of the life you'd grown to love. When your suffering seems to be over-powering you. When you're so, so sick of talking or even thinking about your hurts. Plenty of people wonder what you should say to God when you want to give up on figuring things out and maybe just blame him for the whole bit.

Thankfully, I didn't wonder what to say to God. I knew I wanted to talk with him honestly and openly, the whole way through. And even more thankfully, there wasn't a single thing wrong with that.

During my recovery, a new friend of mine, Liz, who had been in a bad accident of her own, told me about a sermon series that she had been listening to. The series centered on God's work in the book of Job; it had been taught by a pastor from Florida in 2010, over a year before my accident.[13] God brought those sermons to me in Dallas two years after they had first been given, but not surprisingly, that was precisely when I was ready to hear them.

Job is one of the Bible's more familiar books, at least in one sense: Many people know it tells a story of suffering. The most prominent person in the book is Job, after whom the book is named. In almost every chapter, we read about the tremendous pain, loss, and grief this man experienced, all on God's watch. First, thieves and natural disasters come, taking away Job's animals and servants. Next, a house collapses on all of Job's children. Finally, in the middle of Job's mourning, terrible sores appear all over his body. He has to scrape them with shards of pottery, just to get some relief.

It's atrocious stuff. But one of the central points of the book is that God is there, all along. God reminds Job, in fact, that he is infinitely small compared to God, and that in his smallness it isn't Job's place to question God's plan.

After all, the Lord is the creator of everything, the One who poured oceans into place and keeps every single planet in orbit. He's the only great One, and his works are far greater than what humans can even comprehend. This message is delivered to Job powerfully and bluntly, in a fiery speech by God that fills practically four chapters[14] of the book. It's the kind of truth that could *really* sting—except we see that God is not the stinging type. Not at all.

One of the many points that stood out to me in the Job sermon series I listened to is that God doesn't seem to mind when Job is honest about his emotional turmoil. By chapter 3 in the book, Job is already cursing the day he was born[15] and wondering why his mother even bothered to feed him.[16] In chapter 7 he goes on:

> *I cannot keep from speaking.*
> *I must express my anguish.*
> *My bitter soul must complain.*[17]

He continues like this, chapter after chapter, over the course of thirty-five chapters. All that time, God listens to him patiently. If God's response were anything but patience, he could've simply demanded, *Ahem, shut up.*

I can hardly express how encouraging it was for me, in the midst of all my own questions and wonderings and worries, to realize how gentle God was in listening to Job's complaints. What I saw in the Bible gave me confidence that this same God would allow the same kind of emotional honesty from me, too. (Sure, he might have some powerful and blunt reminders for me at some point, but like Job, I probably need them.)

Even though I am exceedingly small before him, God is lovingly willing to hear me out when I need to tell him,

Seriously, OUCH. He is not bothered by my doubts, and he is not put off if I try to give him the third degree. He has nothing to hide.

But here is the point: God's Word held the answer I was looking for.

Yes, God wants all of me, less-than-flattering emotions and minor breakdowns included. Yes, he wants me to know that he is with me and for me, through all of it. No, I don't have to filter or censor myself when I come before God. Yes, I can tell him whatever it is I need to get off my chest, with real and raw feelings to boot.

But the point is even bigger than that: I can know and trust these things and more, because the Bible teaches them clearly.

Honing Our Sheep Skills

When Jesus taught his disciples, he often used analogies comparing himself to a shepherd and people to sheep. At first glance, this might not have seemed all too flattering for the people, because sheep are known to be stubborn and fairly stupid. In particular, they have an impossible time trying to find their own way. They'll wander away from their flock without realizing it, and then they'll just keep walking. Unless somebody is watching out for them and regularly bringing them back to the right path, sheep are long gone.

But with a watchful shepherd, sheep can be excellent at following. Even today, in herding cultures, several different flocks of sheep—hundreds of animals—can be intermingled on a hillside, and yet each sheep in the group will be able to distinguish its shepherd's voice from all the others. The sheep will separate from the rest of the

flocks when they hear their own shepherd calling. And when traveling, sheep can follow commands of a shepherd walking behind them—in other words, they can follow their shepherd when they don't even see him. The directions they take are guided by his words to them.

Jesus said it this way: "They won't follow a stranger; they will run from him because they don't know his voice. . . . My sheep listen to my voice; I know them, and they follow me."[18]

Do you notice what he doesn't say there? He doesn't say, "My sheep listen to my voice, and they know me." He says, "My sheep listen to my voice, and I know them." It isn't the sheep's own smarts, knowing their shepherd's voice, that keeps them safe and well. The sheep are safe and well because their Good Shepherd is wonderful in the ways he knows them.

God knows us. He knows what we need, and he wonderfully takes it upon himself to give it. First and foremost, he knows we need a way to be forgiven, so he gives us forgiveness and life in Jesus. But he also knows that on our own we can't understand how amazing this gift of Jesus is. So he gives us a way to understand. He spells it out clearly, using words. Using *the* Word.

Have you ever thought of the Bible as God's voice? As him coming down to speak to you and me and everyone? That's what it is. The Bible is God's voice, speaking to us like a shepherd would. If we want to grasp what it's telling us, one easy way is to start thinking more like sheep.

Ask yourself: Why do sheep obey their shepherd? Why do they listen for his words? Why do they trust him, even when he's behind them and out of their sight? Why do they run from the others who might try to make them follow?

Here is why: They know from experience that when they walk with their shepherd, he will lead them toward what's good for them and away from what's harmful. He has brought them to their food. He has led them to safe places for rest. He has fought off their predators. He has walked countless journeys with them.

In the same way, if we come to know our Shepherd and his words to us—his Word—we'll find that God's voice in our hearts is our food and our protection. His commands and corrections are for our good, and we can trust them even though we can't see him. Having the Bible with us is a way of having our Shepherd's voice with us:

- seeking us out when we're heading toward trouble
- rescuing us when we're already there
- comforting us when we're hurting
- steering us when we're lost
- helping us see what's wrong with our own path, and helping us want his right one instead

We will always be sheep, always likely to follow our sinfulness and drift from God's ways. But with God's strength, we can let his Word guide us. We can get to know the Bible better and better, in order to follow him more closely. This doesn't make us deserving of his love—what it does instead is prove that his love (which we can *never* deserve) is real to us. Real enough to change us.

Psalm 119:11 says, "I have hidden your word in my heart, that I might not sin against you."[19] By hiding God's Word in our hearts (memorizing it), we can take God's Word with us wherever we go. We never have to wander off alone without it. We take his *actual* words with us— the Good Shepherd's voice, familiar and strong and clear.

Then, when we find ourselves in confusing circumstances, hard times, or beautiful moments, God's words can arm us with clarity, encouragement, praise, or whatever else we might need. Even if that's simply the freedom to complain or question when life gets rough, just as Job did and any of us might need to do.

A beautiful heart wants to know God and gets to know him through his Word.

Discussion Starters

1. Read Psalm 1. What does it have to say about knowing God? How rooted would you say you are? How rooted would you like to be?

2. How often do you have God's Word with you and in your heart? Would you be willing to memorize Psalm 119:11 (opposite page) this week?

3. Following means letting God speak first and *then* responding with action. What's one particular challenge you face, where you need to hear God's voice? What does the Bible have to say about that kind of challenge? (If you're not sure, it's a great idea to ask a trusted pastor or look up some passages with a Christian mentor/friend. Sometimes a simple Internet search can help get you pointed in a useful direction too.)

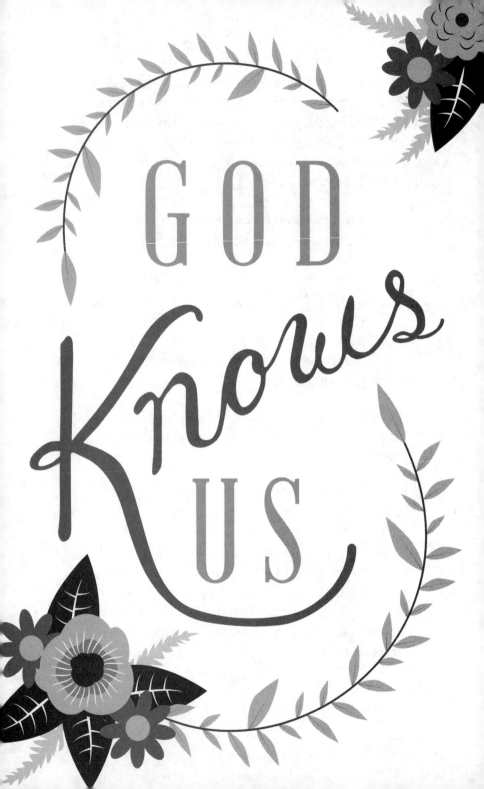

08

A *Heart* That Listens

No. No. No. No.

I had been praying about whether or not to go back to New York. A year after my semester interning with *Gossip Girl* and the Michael Kors fashion showroom, there was an empty summer ahead of me. I wanted to fill it, and I wanted to fill it in my favorite city. But I was having a hard time getting any summer plans to pan out there. No job, no internship, no roommate arrangement, nothing.

And for some reason my parents weren't crazy about me going back, even though they had been absolutely supportive the first time. I couldn't seem to get God on board either. Whenever I prayed and asked him whether I should go back to the city, the answer seemed crystal clear every time: No. No. No. No.

But there was a guy in Dallas, an extremely close

friend of mine, who kept pressuring me to date him. I kept telling him I thought we were better as friends—I was being so blunt it felt almost cruel—but this guy still wouldn't hear me out. It annoyed me that he wouldn't take me seriously. I felt small and insignificant as a result, and I wanted to escape those feelings. Plus I didn't have any jobs or internships or roommates lined up locally to keep me close to home.

So I kept praying and asking God about New York, hoping his answer would change. When that never happened, I went anyway.

I peddled my résumé nearly everywhere in the city. I wasn't picky; any decent job would do—but no matter how many applications I turned in and no matter how many calls I made to follow up, I couldn't manage to get myself hired. It was almost as if the entire city had shut down to me. For a while a journalism opportunity seemed like it might happen, but eventually that fell flat too.

The days passed. I wasn't making any money, and I had nothing productive to do. So a friend and I went to Central Park, where we worked on our tans, and while waiting and hoping that someone would hire me, I met some people along the way.

There were three guys I met and then spent time with that summer. Not one of them was a Christian. The third guy, Brooks, repeatedly asked me to break my commitment to sexual integrity, even though I told him repeatedly I didn't want to. But I still dated him. By the middle of the summer, I was spending nearly every day with him. I liked how I felt when I was with him. It was a nice distraction from more serious things.

This was the most serious thing: My heart wasn't

right, and I knew it. I wasn't focusing on God like I could have been that summer. It's hard to focus on God when you feel like you've blatantly disobeyed him. Instead I was simply going forward and doing my best to settle in the city. That's what I had started out the summer doing, and I didn't have any plans to stop.

But something was about to stop me.

I started getting extremely, inexplicably tired. I couldn't figure out why—I was living a healthy lifestyle, eating well, and balancing my workouts with plenty of relaxation. But I was exhausted constantly. Next I started getting inexplicably dizzy, too.

Around this time, Brittany came to visit me to celebrate our twenty-first birthdays, and she told me that I had zero color in my skin and lips. Later that week, while she and I were making our way around the city, I passed out in the middle of a Times Square subway station and had to be taken by ambulance to the ER.

The doctors did some tests and told me I was probably dehydrated. After the hospital staff had gotten me back on my feet, Brittany and I went back to my apartment, where I drank a lot of water and ate watermelon nonstop. Nothing seemed to improve, though. A few days later, I was at a point where I could barely function. By this time, my mom had been researching my symptoms and options online, and when she heard that things were still getting worse, she basically forced me to go to a doctor she had found.

The new doctor drew some blood for testing. When the results came in the next morning, he called me and told me to immediately come back to his office. He told me my red blood cell count was supposed to be at 12, but mine was at 4.5. He said he was surprised I was still alive.

I ended up in the hospital for four days, having several blood transfusions and endless tests. I even swallowed a tiny camera so doctors could get visual images of my whole digestive tract. By the time my hospital stay was over, we knew that I was bleeding internally and that I had symptoms of malnutrition. But nobody had figured out why the systems in my body were freaking out.

I texted Brooks to let him know. I figured that with grim news like this, he would want to be told. By then he was basically my boyfriend, after all. But when Brooks responded to my text, it would be his last piece of communication to me before I left New York that summer. It was three letters: OMG.

He never checked in, dropped by, asked a single question, or wanted details. He simply stopped spending every day with me, and things were done between us, just like that.

That was the beginning of the end for my stay in the city. I had no choice but to accept that even Brooks was just another letdown in that summer's never-ending pile of them. I had convinced myself that he was the one good thing that had happened to me all season, but the reality was, he didn't even think our relationship was worth "Um, bye."

While I recovered in the hospital, Brittany packed up my New York apartment and took my stuff with her on her return flight to Dallas. My mom had dropped everything and come to the city to be with me, and as soon as I was discharged, we flew back to Texas together. It was earlier than I had intended to leave, but there wasn't a good reason for me to be there anymore. I wasn't sure there ever had been.

How to Hear the Holy Spirit

God used that summer in New York to teach me a lot of valuable lessons, and I'm grateful for them. That said, possibly the biggest lesson God taught me through that trip was that I never should have gone in the first place. I should have listened to the whispers and shouts that were sounding off in my heart, pointing me somewhere else. I know now—I knew then, too—that they were the Holy Spirit speaking to me.

Here's the thing about the Holy Spirit: He's God's gift to believers in Jesus. When Jesus was about to leave the earth and return to his place with God, that's how he introduced the Holy Spirit. He promised his disciples that God was about to give them a gift, and this gift was so important that the disciples were not supposed to leave Jerusalem without it.

A few days later, the Holy Spirit showed up at an event that became known as Pentecost. This was during a busy time in Jerusalem, when multitudes of people from different countries were together in the city for a religious feast. It was in the middle of that melting pot that a powerful and never-before-seen kind of thing happened. Fire shaped like tongues appeared over the Christians' heads, and they began speaking in languages they didn't know.

Imagine that! Skip the Spanish or Greek or Chinese classes, and don't bother with a single vocabulary flashcard. *Poof!*—suddenly you're fluent. And so is the person next to you, and the person next to them too, all in different languages. That's how it happened that day.

The visiting pilgrims' ears perked up, don't you think? Of course they did. And as this captive audience listened, the early Christians shared with them the story of Jesus. The Holy Spirit had demolished barriers so the best news ever could be spoken plainly and understood. God's gift had come.[20] What happened on Pentecost introduced the world to how the Holy Spirit works. He speaks the language of God's heart and helps our own hearts understand it.

But how can we know when the Holy Spirit is speaking to us? How can we expect him to speak to us in the first place? Here are some truths from the Bible about that:

- **Because the Holy Spirit *is* God, he will never guide us toward something that doesn't match God's Word.** If the Bible says no, we will not hear the Holy Spirit saying yes. And vice versa.
- **The Holy Spirit is a promise we can depend on.** Jesus said that if we obey his commandments, God will give us the Holy Spirit, who will never leave us (see John 14:15-17).
- **The Holy Spirit will drive us away from sin.** The apostle Paul wrote it this way: "Let the Holy Spirit guide your lives. Then you won't be doing what your sinful nature craves."[21] Often we try to tell ourselves that we're hearing the Holy Spirit when *really* what we're hearing is our own emotion or selfishness. If we're tuned into only our own feelings and desires, we're in danger of falling into sin. Our hearts have little idols in them, remember?
- **The Holy Spirit helps in our weakness** (Romans 8:26). He is able to give us strength to overcome the sinfulness in our hearts and to follow God boldly, even when we feel like we might not be able to.
- **The Holy Spirit fills our hearts with God's love**

(Romans 5:5). Listening to the Holy Spirit will remind us of God's love. We will want as much of that love as possible, and the more we drink it up, the more we'll seek to give God glory.

- **Life in the Holy Spirit includes goodness and peace and joy** (Romans 14:17). Even if the Holy Spirit guides us in ways that seem difficult or in ways we wouldn't have chosen ourselves, he gives us a sense of undeniable calm and bubbling delight. Hard times are still good when we let him lead us.

- **Like Jesus, the Holy Spirit is part of God himself.** That means he exhibits God's character perfectly. He loves fully. And he wants only the best for those he loves. Like all God's gifts, there is no reason to *not* want this one.

- **The Holy Spirit is in our corner.** Some translations of the Bible call the Holy Spirit "the Comforter" and "the Advocate." Jesus told his disciples in John 14:26 that the Holy Spirit would remind them of everything he had taught them. There's no question that includes comfort for when we've messed up—a welcoming embrace when we've lost our way.

A beautiful heart listens for the Holy Spirit.

Discussion Starters

1. What's one weakness in your life where you can rely on the Holy Spirit for strength?

2. Are there emotions or areas of selfishness that you find easier to listen to than the Holy Spirit? How can you trust the Holy Spirit to outshine those things in your life?

3. Do you trust that God will lead you toward only what's best for you? Why or why not? If not, what do you think is wrong about your perspective?

09

A *Heart* That Heals

One Girl, Two Trials:
A Sorrow Story

My friend Casey's dad died during our senior year of high school. It was a heart attack, and nobody had seen it coming. The death hit like a stick of dynamite in the middle of their family: quickly, loudly, painfully, and powerfully. Relationships exploded at the center, and in an instant, what had been whole about their family became fragmented, flung apart in several pieces.

The day before it happened, Casey was living happily in one of the coolest families around. Her parents had a great marriage, and they were really close with all three of their kids. That was a Saturday in mid-September. On Sunday, Casey's mom was suddenly a widow, and along with her three teenagers, she was missing Dan Novak desperately.

When you lose someone you love, that alone is enough to make life feel like it's coming off the hinges. But losing

a dad and a husband was just the first tragedy this family had to face. A few years after her dad died, Casey's brother Cody was diagnosed with a rare form of cancer on his tailbone. The family's first grief was still ripe and fresh as anything, and now they wondered if they were being given a second dose.

How would they respond? How would they get through?

Casey and I weren't particularly close when all that started, but she and my sister were, so through Brittany we always maintained a link, even after graduating. I could see that after Casey's dad died and then again during the first part of Cody's illness, she withdrew a little. She almost seemed to be pushing some people away.

First of all, who could blame her? It takes a long time to start healing when your hurts are huge. And second, no matter how things might have looked from the outside, ultimately Casey was healing in the right way. She was learning to put her pain in God's hands and to trust that he would care for her best.

She learned to look to God for comfort when she felt like her sadness was closing in. She learned to ask him for peace and calm when she felt angrier than ever. She learned to seek God's fulfillment when her dad's absence felt like a gaping hole. She learned to pray and believe that God's answers made sense, even when she couldn't begin to understand them.

In all of those things, she became a stunning source of encouragement to others in their pain, including me in mine.

After my accident, I had some days when I struggled to believe that the pain I was feeling could *ever* result in

anything good, and on those days Casey was there to remind me of God's faithfulness. When I was dealing with insecurities about how the accident had changed me, Casey would promise to pray. The next day and then again a few days later, she would check in: "I'm praying for you in this. How are you doing? Are things getting better?"

Her care was gentle and firm, reliable and on purpose. It was exactly what I needed from a friend, and she knew that perfectly, because she had needed care like that once too. I can't express how thankful I am that God has given me Casey, someone who knows from experience that hurts don't have to be roadblocks to faith. Someone whose love and care remind others of that fact on a regular basis.

About a year ago on the anniversary of her dad's death, Casey posted a photo online of some flowers she had received that day. Her caption acknowledged that it was a hard day, but you also couldn't miss the core belief that's now rooting her: "Miss my dad, but thankful for a faithful and loving heavenly Father."

Pain Is a Gift

Everyone has hurts and hardships in life. The pain we feel, especially in our toughest times, will either make us bitter and numb, or it will make us better. Pain makes us better when we look to God in our pain and learn to let him heal us. When we do that, we come to understand how pain can be an incredible gift.

First, though, we have to remind ourselves about the best thing in life. It's not comfort or pleasure or health or a long life or success or security or getting/keeping a lot of stuff. The best thing for us, bar none, is knowing God and finding life through his Son, Jesus. That is what brings us ultimate comfort, ultimate pleasure, ultimate joy, and the only real security. Anything—yes, *anything*—that gets us to that is magnificent.

Pain is a gift because pain shows us where our strength and control ends. It puts us in a position where we're quicker to be desperate for God. *Lord, this hurts like crazy, and I can't make it stop. Please comfort me or make it stop.* Without hurts staring us in the face, often we forget to turn to God. Often we get lost in ourselves and in other earthly things—less important things. *Lord, this pain is way too big for me to handle on my own. I can't get through it without you. I need you.*

Pain can be blinding, though, and when we're hurting a lot we can begin to doubt that God will use this pain for our best. Sometimes we want to believe lies: that God is punishing us, that he doesn't care about us, that we haven't been good enough to earn his favor, or that he couldn't possibly exist at all. None of that is possible, given what we know of God:

> He already took our punishment.
> He cares deeply for us.
> His love isn't based on our behavior.
> He left heaven so he could exist right here on earth
>   with us, feeling firsthand all the most terrible
>   kinds of pain.

The pain-is-punishment idea doesn't hold up, no matter how much we might think it. No, pain is an invitation. It's an invitation for us to seek this God who loves us so much. When we seek him, we will find him—the Bible promises that! And in finding God, we find everything that is comforting and good. Even when life stings. Because

God is in the business of redeeming pain: taking something that seems awful and turning it into good.

Here's one example of how that happens. In Psalm 13 we find King David in a tough spot. That's obvious from the first two verses:

> O LORD, how long will you forget me? Forever?
>> How long will you look the other way?
> How long must I struggle with anguish in my soul,
>> with sorrow in my heart every day?
> How long will my enemy have the upper hand?[22]

David feels abandoned, at risk, and weak. His emotions are full of turmoil and overwhelming sadness. It seems like he has been feeling this way for a long time. But David doesn't keep his focus on the hard times he's in. He turns to God for rescue and asks for the help he knows God can give:

> Turn and answer me, O LORD my God!
>> Restore the sparkle to my eyes, or I will die.
> Don't let my enemies gloat, saying, "We have defeated
>> him!"
> Don't let them rejoice at my downfall.[23]

What we see next is a remarkable shift. After expressing his trust in God, David seems to have a total change of outlook. In fact, the final two verses of Psalm 13 are praise:

> But I trust in your unfailing love.
>> I will rejoice because you have rescued me.
> I will sing to the LORD
>> because he is good to me.[24]

Do you see what happened there? David's circumstances haven't changed at all, but he sings as if they have. *You have rescued me,* he says to God. *You have!* That's past tense, even though nothing has changed. In other words, David is either remembering a time in the past when God rescued him, or he's so sure that God *will* rescue him that he's already talking about it in past tense. Either way, the reason for David's confidence is obvious: *I will sing to the LORD because he is good to me.*

How do we find God in our pain? It's simple. We seek him. We look for him in our lives, and we remind ourselves of his character and faithfulness. We read the Bible and pray, believing God is full of comfort and compassion. We let our hurts lead us to his healing.

The easiest, breeziest times in life are often the most shallow, and times of struggle are filled with loads of depth. When we choose to feel cheated by our pain, we miss out on some of the richness that God has to offer us through it. Pain is a gift, but *it* unwraps *us*; it opens us up and shows us how empty and helpless we are without God and his goodness. In that way, it can lead us straight to praise.

A beautiful heart responds to pain
by trusting in God's healing.

Discussion Starters

1. Read Psalm 34:17-19. What does this passage tell us about how God responds to our hurts and troubles?

2. What kind of pain are you facing, and how does that struggle reveal your need for God?

3. David asked for the help he knew God could give. In what way(s) can you ask God to be your help through trials or suffering? In what way(s) can you move forward with praise, remembering and trusting that God has been good to you?

SHARING YOUR FAITH IS SIMPLY
TALKING ABOUT THE GOD WHO KNOWS
AND CARES ABOUT YOU WITH PEOPLE
YOU KNOW AND CARE ABOUT.

10

A *Heart* That Overflows

Connor and I ran into each other after dinner one night in downtown Dallas. I was with some of my friends, and he was with some of his friends, and after talking for a while, our two circles formed one big group and ended up hanging out together for the rest of the evening. Connor had attended my high school for a while, where he was a few years ahead of me, but that night in Dallas was the first time I really got to know him.

In high school, Connor had become somewhat legendary for getting suspended. Apparently he had a habit of breaking school rules, and he was kicked out of class almost as often as he was allowed in. (He might've even been out *more* than he was in.) On the night we met, though, Connor had graduated from college and put high school far behind him. I found him to be intelligent,

exciting, and fun, and our interests aligned right away. When we talked, we seemed to be on the same wavelength. Needless to say, we hit it off. And we were in the middle of summer, so we both had some spare time on our hands. Beginning that night, we began hanging out on a pretty regular basis.

I found out rather quickly that Connor had taken religion courses at college. They had become extremely influential in his thoughts about life and faith. But what he had been studying was a far cry from anything we had studied together at our Christian high school. Connor no longer bought into the idea of a clearly defined, personal God, like the Bible talks about. He didn't believe that Jesus is the Savior or that people need Jesus in order to be saved.

Now he believed that "God" was just a big spirit-world that existed in and around everything: Every tree has some "God" in it; the stars have some "God" in them; a frog has some "God" in it; and somewhere in Connor and in you, me, and everyone else there's some "God" too.

We talked a lot about faith and religion that summer. (One night, we talked about it for probably two hours straight!) In those conversations, often his comments would go something like this: "I believe that 'God' is *such-and-such* a way, because *this certain book* by *this well-known philosopher* says *this and that* about the universe and matter and particles, and that means *this, that, and the other* about religion, and it really makes perfect sense, don't you see?" (I'm not making fun of Connor here; I simply can't remember the specific kinds of information he would give. The point is, in one way or another, it always sounded studious and very smart.)

Connor is a well-spoken, intellectual person. When we talked, sometimes he made spot-on observations—some good, some bad—about Christians. He made some excellent points about the importance of faith. But when he spoke about God, it didn't match what I saw in the Bible, and it didn't match the kind of work I knew the Lord had been doing in my life and in the world around me. I knew in my heart that his view of God wasn't true.

Most of the time, I couldn't respond to Connor by quoting a famous philosopher of my own, and I usually didn't have much to say about particles and matter in the universe. But I had confidence in who God is, so I could reply to Connor with confidence. Usually it went something like this: "Well, I don't know—I'm actually going to have to look that up, but I don't believe that to be true, what you're saying." Then I would talk a little about God's good news—how it's the hope of the world, and how it had changed my heart.

Connor always seemed intrigued when his scholarly opinions and literary perspectives about faith didn't sway me. I'm sure he was used to people finding his points and arguments convincing, and I could tell that his curiosity was triggered whenever I didn't agree that his perspective was on-target. That's one of the reasons why I enjoyed talking with him so much about faith; he was curious. When someone who doesn't believe in God is curious, it means there's potentially ripe soil for whatever faith seeds God is using you to sow.

How to Share Our Faith, and Why We Should
Sometimes when people think about "sharing faith" with others, the first ideas that come to mind are of cross-cultural mission trips or street-evangelism teams. Those

are both good examples of sharing faith with others. Still, more often than not, sharing your faith is simply talking about the God who knows and cares about you with people you know and care about. When you've seen how much the God of the Bible knows you and cares about you, it's only natural to want to share his story as often as possible.

John 4 tells the story of one woman who, after meeting Jesus, did exactly that. This woman, like my friend Connor, had potentially ripe soil where seeds of faith could be sown. Like Connor, she knew what it was like to have a less-than-excellent reputation. But unlike Connor, this woman—because of her history and ethnicity—wasn't at all familiar with being taken seriously.

The woman was a Samaritan. That means she belonged to a group of people who lived in a part of Israel called Samaria. Long before Jesus came to the world, a foreign king had brought non-Jewish people into that region, and over the years the Jews from Samaria had married them and adopted some of their customs. Because of that, Samaritans became outcasts among pretty much everybody. To the Jews, Samaritans weren't Jewish enough, and to the non-Jews, Samaritans were too Jewish. It wasn't uncommon for Jews, when they traveled in Israel, to make a detour around Samaria, avoiding even walking through it. This was not an easy bypass; it took crossing a river twice!

So the woman in John 4 was already an outcast because of her ethnicity. Along with that, though, she was an outcast because of her choices. The Bible tells us she had been married five different times, and now she was living with a man she wasn't married to. That kind of relationship history would be on the wild side even today—back then, it was complete scandal.

Jesus and this woman met each other at a well around noon. Jesus was at the well because he had been traveling and was thirsty. In a desert-nation like Israel, noon would have been one of the hottest times of the day, so it made sense for him to be there. But for the woman to come to the well to draw water at that time of day was odd. Usually women drew water during the coolest hours of the day, but there she was in the hottest heat. Why? Many Bible scholars suggest that this woman went to the well at noon because she wanted to avoid others, who would probably look down on her.

But Jesus (the full Jew who was also perfect) talked with her (the obviously sinful partial Jew) naturally and kindly. He didn't treat her like an outcast; instead, he asked for her help in getting a drink. Then he began telling her about the gift of eternal life that God offers. He also brought up her living situation, helping the woman see that although they had never met, Jesus already knew her deeply. He saw her ethnicity and knew her sin, and neither one kept him from her. Then Jesus encouraged the woman, telling her that anyone—even she!—could worship in God's Kingdom. In God's Kingdom, he said, there are no silly dividing lines that turn people into outcasts. All you need is the ability to worship in spirit and in truth. He told her, "The Father is looking for those who will worship him that way."[25]

Just imagine how invigorating those words must have been to a woman who probably felt like she'd only ever be a social discard. They must have been like the freshest, coolest water on a scalding-hot day. She could belong.

The woman drank up Jesus' message in gigantic gulps. Then she—the same one who had gone to the well at the best time to avoid contact with anybody—ran back to her village and told everyone. Suddenly she was no longer dodging other people. She was seeking them out, all of them, in order to share God's thirst-ending gift with them. Jesus' living water was bubbling up in her so much that she couldn't help but let it overflow.

Here's the thing about this passage: When we read it, I think sometimes we forget that we are the Samaritan woman too. Our hearts are just as sinful as hers was, no matter how obedient or appropriate we might look on the outside. Jesus knows the sin in our hearts, just like he knew hers, and he could call us out on our sin as easily. But just like he did with this woman, he sits with us, and instead of focusing on the ways our sin makes us outcasts, he welcomes us to himself.

His living water should taste just as amazing to us as it did to her. And we should be every bit as eager to let it overflow. (That, I think, is one reason I loved talking about God with Connor.)

Are we amazed by God's gift to us? Does it make us giddy to share our faith with others, even people we might otherwise avoid? Do we really believe that this water is so alive, it's impossible to hold it in?

A beautiful heart overflows to others with the message of God's love and forgiveness.

Discussion Starters

1. Have you avoided talking with others about God and faith? If so, whom have you avoided? Why?

2. This chapter talks about how *we* are the Samaritan woman. What does that mean?

3. Read Matthew 28:16-20. These are the last words Jesus spoke to his followers before he went back to be with God. What does he tell them to do? How does he encourage them? How can we be challenged and encouraged by this too?

Part Three

Your Obedient Heart

A *beautiful*
heart
sees
the **sin**
that
entangles it.

11

A *Heart* That Sees Sin

My Faulty Radar:
A Checklist Story

$\mathcal{M}$y heart was pounding because I knew Chrissie would want to know about my sins.

I was in high school, and along with a bunch of other girls my age, I was in a small group led by an adult from our church. That adult was Chrissie. Every other week or so, each of us would meet one-on-one with Chrissie to talk specifically about our own personal life and faith. At every one of those meetings, the pair of us would pray about sins.

"How can I be praying for you personally this week?" Chrissie would ask. "What have you been struggling with?" That was what cued my nerves every time.

Since the other girls in our group were my friends, I knew I could probably guess at some of their confessions for the week.

"I caved in to peer pressure at my friend's house last week," one girl might have said.

"I'm worried about going too far with my boyfriend," another might have admitted.

"I've been really disrespectful to my parents."

"I thought about cheating on some assignments the other day."

I figured that everybody else probably had great answers for Chrissie's sin question, with perfect problems to be prayed about. That's why my heart always pounded so badly when she asked me about mine. It seems silly to me now, thinking about it, but back then, most days I genuinely didn't think there was anything for me to confess. I wanted to have some obvious sin to tell Chrissie about, but I would run through my mental checklist and come up with nothing.

- ✓ I don't cuss.
- ✓ I don't drink.
- ✓ I read my Bible.
- ✓ I haven't lied recently.
- ✓ I've never had sex.
- ✓ I have good friendships.
- ✓ I'm usually not mean to people.
- ✓ I don't intentionally do anything rude.
- ✓ I respect my parents most of the time.

So, *shoot.* By the end of my checklist, I felt like I had run out of options. I couldn't come up with any good sins that applied—but I really wanted to have something! And I thought I *should* have something. So on those days when it was my turn to meet with Chrissie, the "something" I told her was completely made up.

I'd tell her that I wasn't waking up to spend time with God at the beginning of the day. I'd tell her I hadn't been

kind in a conversation with Brittany. I'd tell her I didn't handle a situation well with the guy I was dating.

Obviously I never considered the fact that on a regular basis I was lying to my youth leader and that every one of those lies came straight from my sinful heart. Back then, the idea of a sinful heart wasn't really on my radar. It had never occurred to me that I should even think about it, much less keep it at the top of my checklist.

Hidden Greed and a Father's Love

We read in Luke 15 that during Jesus' ministry, many religious people got upset with him because they saw him hanging out with sinners. They complained that Jesus was allowing even tax collectors (notoriously selfish, greedy people) to spend time with him!

In response to their complaints, Jesus told some parables. Parables are stories that have been invented to express meaning. These parables were meant to show what sin *actually* looks like.

One of the parables Jesus told was a story of a father and his two sons. The younger son in the parable is disobedient and selfish, and the older son is seemingly good. But not everything in the parable is how it might initially come across.

The parable starts out horribly. The younger son went to his father and asked for his part of the family inheritance. Since an inheritance was what someone would get only after the father was no longer living, what this younger son basically said was, "Dad, I wish you were dead. All I care about is your money."

The father didn't have to do this, but he divided up his household and belongings so he could give his younger son the money he had asked for. After that, the son promptly left home and moved far away, where he wasted his money like a fool. The rest of the younger son's story goes like this:

About the time his money ran out, a great famine swept over the land, and he began to starve. He persuaded a local farmer to hire him, and the man sent him into his fields to feed the pigs. The young man became so hungry that even the pods he was feeding the pigs looked good to him. But no one gave him anything.

When he finally came to his senses, he said to himself, "At home even the hired servants have food enough to spare, and here I am dying of hunger! I will go home to my father and say, 'Father, I have sinned against both heaven and you, and I am no longer worthy of being called your son. Please take me on as a hired servant.'"

So he returned home to his father. And while he was still a long way off, his father saw him coming. Filled with love and compassion, he ran to his son, embraced him, and kissed him. His son said to him, "Father, I have sinned against both heaven and you, and I am no longer worthy of being called your son."

But his father said to the servants, "Quick! Bring the finest robe in the house and put it on him. Get a ring for his finger and sandals for his feet. And kill the calf we have been fattening. We must celebrate with a feast, for this son of mine was dead and has now returned to life. He was lost, but now he is found." So the party began.[26]

That's the familiar part of the story—the part where the father (representing God) races to accept his wayward child back home. But that's not the end of this parable. There is more to the story and more to the meaning.

In the middle of the homecoming celebration, the older, responsible brother comes home from his work in the fields. Noticing all the music and dancing, he asks a servant what's going on. The servant tells him his brother is back, safe and sound, and their father has killed a fattened calf to celebrate.

Now, if the older brother in this story cared about what his father cared about, we could expect that he would be delighted too. His father had thought one of his sons was long gone, and he had endured a painful break in their relationship. But now the son was back, and things were healed! Even if the older son wasn't over the moon to see his younger brother again, he could at least be happy for the sake of their father. Right?

But he's not. He throws a fit, refusing to go inside. This causes enough of a scene that it forces the father to stop celebrating and leave the party so he can beg his older son to come in. The son still refuses. "All these years," he tells his father, "I've slaved for you and never once refused to do a single thing you told me to. And in all that time you never gave me even one young goat for a feast with my friends. Yet when this son of yours comes back after squandering your money on prostitutes, you celebrate by killing the fattened calf!" (verses 29-30).

There is something happening here that's easy to miss.

When the older son talks to his father about "*your* money," what he's really saying is "mine, mine, *mine*." Remember, the father had already divided up his household and had given the younger son his full share. All the money and belongings that remained—including the fine robe the younger brother was now wearing, the ring on his finger, the sandals on his feet, and the choice beef in his belly—were supposed to belong to the older brother one day.

Part of what the older brother is saying, standing there ticked off and stubborn outside the house, is this: "I deserve far more than you've ever given me, and now you're taking what *is* mine and giving it to *him* instead!"

On what is probably one of the most joyous days of the father's life, this son doesn't care one bit. He wants no part in rejoicing with his dad. He wants his stuff, and he's irate there hasn't been more of it.

When Jesus ends this parable, the older son is still outside the door. Unlike his irresponsible younger brother, the older one hasn't reconciled with his father. He hasn't seen that he and his brother share a similar heart. The greed that drove his brother to disrespect their father by asking for an early payout is the same sort of greed that is now causing his own outrage.[27]

That's how sin goes. Romans 3:23 tells us that "everyone has sinned; we all fall short of God's glorious standard." So those of us who think we're doing pretty well should try looking a little deeper. As the parable of the two sons shows, sin can hide carefully and craftily, even under what looks like faithful obedience.

If we think of ourselves as fairly obedient and not very sinful, it's probably *not* because we've been spending a lot of time thinking about the lavishness of God's forgiveness. It's probably *not* because we love God so purely that all we want is his pleasure. More likely, it's because our sinful hearts have made an idol out of being good people. Or maybe we idolize being successful at things, and obedience is just another A+ for us. Or perhaps, deep down, we idolize feeling better than others and keeping others down. Or possibly it's simply that we idolize our own interests and thoughts, so we haven't bothered reading our Bibles enough to realize what God has to say about sin— which is that every one of us has *plenty* of sins to share about and pray for.

> *A beautiful heart sees the sin*
> *that entangles it.*

Discussion Starters

1. Have you ever mistakenly thought that obedience is the same as sinlessness? What does the parable of the two sons suggest about that?

2. Do you think that there are things you want from God (blessings, influence, comfort, a good name, etc.) more than you actually want God himself? What's one of the greedy idols in your own heart?

3. Read Luke 15:31-32. What does the father's response to his son tell us about the father? What hope does that help us have, as humans whose hearts are gripped by sin?

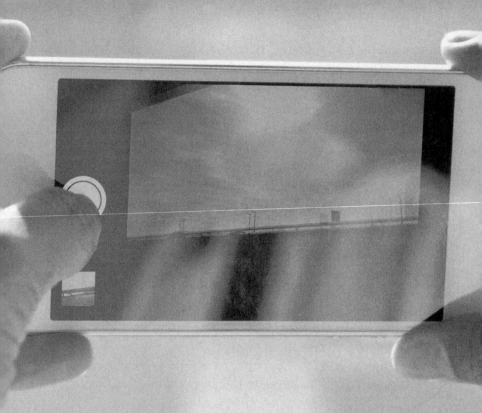

LOVING GOD TAKES OUR FOCUS

OFF OURSELVES AND WHAT WE WANT,

PUTTING OUR ATTENTION

ON GOD AND WHAT HE WANTS.

12

A *Heart* That Repents

Calling My Sister:
A Selfishness Story

"**I** need Brittany."

I can't tell you how many times I cried out for my twin sister during the early days of my recovery. I called out for her in times when my physical pain seemed almost over-whelming. In times when I felt like I might be toppled by all the adjustments and changes going on. On days when the hard work of healing seemed too daunting. On days when I didn't want to get out of bed.

When I didn't know what to do or how to do it, often Brittany was the best comfort and the brightest encour-agement to me. She would come over to our parents' house and sit with me, and somehow all the unsettledness in me would settle. I could relax, breathe deeply, and feel a sense of peace.

As time went on and I entered a new phase of recov-ery, I continued to rely on Brittany, only in different ways.

For a while, Brittany and her husband, Shaun, hosted me at their place every weekend to give me a change of pace and scenery.

I'd spend a night or two, and during the days we'd do something simple, like relaxing and hanging out. Brittany and Shaun have a giant beanbag chair that can fit all three of us. Often we'd rent a couple of silly movies and cozy up on it with some ice cream or chocolate (or both). We'd laugh and joke and talk for hours. It was a blast, and it always felt like precisely what I needed.

In most ways, none of this was surprising. I had known for a long time that Brittany (and Shaun, too) would give up nearly anything in life to be there for someone else. Brittany is just that way, always giving to others generously and quietly behind the scenes. Still, I was taken aback by how meaningful Brittany's service was to me. It almost felt unfamiliar.

After thinking for a while about that, I realized why: Brittany's love seemed unfamiliar because I hadn't really appreciated it in a long time. I had been overlooking important parts of Brittany's life for a while.

In the months and maybe even years before my accident, I had been caught up in my own interests and career goals—at the time, mostly launching an online magazine. I had been arranging partnerships, making appointments, researching, promoting, and getting a website up and running. I *hadn't* been paying much attention to Brittany, one of the closest people in the world to me and one of the people I claim to care about most. In fact, after her wedding I hadn't had much more than a glimpse of what her life as a wife was like.

Then came the accident. During my healing and recovery, Brittany's love for me was steadfast and constant. Even though it must've been immensely chaotic and straining for her, watching someone she loves endure trauma, she was always at the hospital, always sacrificing, always holding strong amid uncertainty, always showing concern.

I had been selfish and had overlooked her; she had been selfless and had worked to notice my every need.

That realization was powerfully convicting, and I knew I needed to do something about it. Specifically, I needed to do two somethings. One was between Brittany and me: I needed to reach out to her, apologizing and seeking forgiveness for whatever hurts or division my selfishness had caused. The other didn't have much to do with Brittany specifically, even though it was my relationship with her that had made me realize this step was necessary.

This other "something" would go deeper. Because although repentance can happen in a relationship between people, repentance should never *just* happen between people. There should always be the one step that goes further.

A Complicated Scheme and a Single Sin

In 2 Samuel 11, we read a story about David, king of Israel. It begins when, while walking on his roof, he sees a woman bathing. David asks about her, only to find out she's married—but her husband is away serving in the Israelite army. So David summons her to his palace and sleeps with her. Soon after, she finds out she's pregnant (by him) and tells him so.

David brings the woman's husband, Uriah, back from war, hoping Uriah will spend a night with his wife. But Uriah refuses because his comrades in the army are still living in tents. So David sends him back to battle, telling a commander to put him in the heat of the fight, then to leave him stranded there so he'll be killed. All this happens. The wife gets the news, and when she's done mourning her husband's death, David marries her. Their baby is born in the palace.

After all this, God sends his prophet Nathan to bring David a message from God. Nathan goes to King David and tells him a story about two men, one of them rich and one of them poor. The rich man has flocks, herds, and property, but the poor man has only one lamb. The poor man loves his one lamb and even lets it eat off the table with his family. Then one day the rich man needs to prepare a feast for a guest. Instead of killing one of his own animals for food, the rich man kills the poor man's beloved lamb.

By this point in the story, David is enraged. He tells Nathan that the rich man's sin is so awful that he must pay back the poor man by giving him four lambs. He also tells the prophet that "any man who would do such a thing deserves to die!"[28]

This is where Nathan delivers the message he was sent to bring: "You are that man!" he tells David.[29] He rebukes the king, reminding David that God has been unspeakably generous to him already. He tells David that if all his riches weren't enough, God would've given David even more. Still, David went against God, taking another man's wife and having the man killed. As a result of what David has done, Nathan tells him that tragedies and terrible things will happen in the royal family.

How does David respond? After all that he has done and after the verbal lashing he has just received, he doesn't appear to have much to say. It almost seems too

simplistic—in English, it's only six words: "I have sinned against the LORD."[30]

David let lust grow in his heart until he plotted an affair, and then he schemed to try to cover it up. When that didn't work, he sabotaged the army in his care, betraying his nation and committing murder in order to hide everything. And all he has to say is that he has sinned against the Lord? What about the ways he sinned against everybody else?

But David's perspective *is* right. We can get a glimpse of that by reading Psalm 51, which was written by David about his visit from Nathan. Parts of the psalm go like this:

> *Have mercy on me, O God,*
> *because of your unfailing love.*
> *Because of your great compassion,*
> *blot out the stain of my sins. . . .*
> *For I recognize my rebellion;*
> *it haunts me day and night.*
> *Against you, and you alone, have I sinned;*
> *I have done what is evil in your sight. . . .*
> *Purify me from my sins, and I will be clean;*
> *wash me, and I will be whiter than snow. . . .*
> *Create in me a clean heart, O God.*
> *Renew a loyal spirit within me.*
>
> PSALM 51:1, 3-4, 7, 10

It's not that David is ignoring other people—in fact, in later verses of Psalm 51 David talks about singing God's praise and teaching God's ways to others. So we know David is thinking of how his actions influence those around him. He isn't ignoring others at all. Instead, his heart is laser-focused on the way he has rebelled against God.

He's looking intently there because sin against God is at the center of his wrongs against others.

That's how the story always goes.

When we love God, it doesn't fit the puzzle to be heartless toward others. Loving God takes our focus off ourselves and what *we* want, putting our attention on God and what *he* wants. And when we're looking at what God wants, we'll give our best for the sake of others, like he did. We won't take from others, wanting more for ourselves—that demonstrates the opposite of God's values.

Of course, we can't love God perfectly. Our sinful hearts make that impossible. That's why repentance will always be necessary. And that's why it's worthwhile to keep an eye on our human relationships—they can be great indicators of what's going on in our hearts.

Are we hurting people? Are we stealing from their joy, attention, material stuff, relationships, efforts, reputations, or rewards? What does that say about how ungrateful and untrusting we are toward God for what we *really* need? What does that suggest about how we see him? Usually the answers to those last two questions will deserve most of our concentration, because *those* will show us how we need to repent before God himself.

It doesn't have to be a complicated thing, to recognize that our wrongs against others can reveal our sin against God. I love a story my pastor, Matt, tells about this kind of thing. One day, while talking to his young son, Reid, he used an unnecessarily harsh tone. Later that night, when tucking Reid in, he asked for forgiveness. "Buddy, I'm really sorry I handled it that way. I'm just a sinful person, but the Lord has shown me that he loves me. I want to do my best to remember that and to show this love to you too."

A beautiful heart repents first
and foremost to God.

Discussion Starters

1. One of the ways we hurt others is by stealing from them, whether their joy, their attention, their material stuff, their relationships, their efforts, their reputations, or their rewards. What are some other ways we might hurt people by stealing from them?

2. What's one thing you've recently taken for yourself at someone else's expense? How does that demonstrate your rebellion against God? How would repentance before God change you and affect this situation?

3. How does turning our focus to God help us love other people?

We begin to *get* who God is

when we

CHANGE

for the better.

13

A *Heart* That Rests

So Much Quiet: A Story of Steps

*J*ust a handful of months after my bad summer in New York ended, it was a quiet springtime in Dallas for me. I had graduated from college in December, a semester ahead of schedule, so most of my friends were still either living on campus or going to school somewhere out of town. On top of that, both Brittany and one of my closest Dallas friends were out of the country, studying abroad. That meant that even on weekends (when I typically would've hung out with them), I had plenty of time on my hands. I had a waitressing job and a few projects on my calendar, but there was still a whole lot of alone time in my schedule.

Would it be *bored* time? At first I wasn't sure. But it didn't take long for me to see that time alone was exactly what I needed. Time alone gave me space for long

stretches of thinking, and I had more than enough thinking to do.

My second stay in New York had opened my eyes to some patterns of sin in my life, and I wasn't sure how I should deal with them. Although I knew the Lord and loved him, that summer I had repeatedly made horrible decisions about how I spent my time and who I dated. I had never been so flippant about my social life or my romantic life, and I couldn't figure out how those kinds of decisions had become so appealing to me. I had a hunch that getting to the bottom of my confusion about it would require a little digging.

I knew of a program at my church called Steps to Recovery, which is basically a plan for taking a hard look at sin and the consequences of sin in your life. It's a sixteen-week process with twelve steps, modeled somewhat after Alcoholics Anonymous. People I knew who had been through Steps had recommended it highly, too, so I signed up for the spring session.

Steps took commitment, and it took time. I was assigned a mentor, and every week I'd meet with a small group of other young women first, then together we'd go hear a message about that week's topic. There was individual homework given for each week, and toward the end of the program, each of us was responsible to take an inventory of five broad categories of sin. Imagine filling five pages of paper (in small print!) with remembrances of your sins, reflections on why you sinned, and observations about what had resulted from those sins. That's what we did. In *detail*.

A final step in the program was to meet with my mentor one-on-one and read my entire inventory out loud. During that step, the point was that I wasn't really reading it to her; I was reading it to God and to myself, with my mentor's presence for support. Part of the intent behind this was that confessing sin before God lifts the weight of that sin. It takes the burden away. And having a mentor there is good accountability to make sure you make it through the whole inventory, all the way to the burden being lifted.

It was the coolest thing, going through Steps and eventually reading that inventory out loud. I don't know how to describe it other than to say that an enormous release happened. I had been holding tightly to many things—certain patterns of sin, confusion and guilt over my sins, broken relationships that I had caused with my sin—sometimes without even knowing I was doing it. Suddenly I felt free. I felt strengthened to change repeating sinful behaviors. I felt clear on what some of my weaknesses were and how I could seek God's help in overcoming them. I felt like I could approach people I had hurt in the past, ask for forgiveness, and move forward with even *more* release.

Steps changed me more than I can say, probably for the rest of my life. I'm so glad for the ways God used it to speak to me that spring. And I'm grateful that he gave me a season full of so much quiet in the first place. It created the perfect space for me to listen for God and hear. The perfect place to be changed.

Dusty Sandals and Letting Life Stop
"Be still, and know that I am God!"[31] That's God's message in Psalm 46, in the midst of a whole passage about times of trouble, coming earthquakes, crumbling mountains, nations in chaos, oceans that roar, waters that surge, and spears and shields being used in war. This psalm gives a picture of turmoil all around—catastrophes

everywhere—yet the writer responds to the mess by reminding us that "the God of Israel is our fortress" (verse 11). It's God's own voice in the psalm that tells us to "Be still."

Most of us aren't good at stillness. At *really* stopping. Sure, we might be good at sitting at home and watching mindless movies or going to coffee shops or reading thoughtful books or listening to background music—most of us are great at that kind of thing—but what I'm talking about here is stopping all that stuff too. Stillness brings an actual halt to our regular activities and mental pace, enough to home in on *only* God's works and tune our ears to only his words.

Think about it: What's happening in Psalm 46 is the kind of stuff that speeds people up. We react hurriedly to disasters, we rush to reorder things after bedlam, and we certainly wouldn't just stand around doing nothing if our city were under attack and our lives were in danger. But that's exactly what God's voice in the psalm tells us to do. One translation of the Bible puts it like this: "*Cease striving and know that I am God.*"[32] Cease striving. In other words, quit focusing on your own efforts, because your own efforts are not what you need most right now. God is what you need most.

It's hard to hear God when we keep the rest of our life's noise turned up megaphone-loud all the time. It's hard to absorb an important message (and all God's messages are important) when our calendars are crowded endlessly. It's hard to know him when we're not willing to take our focus off everything else every now and then, in order to actually look him in the eye.

Before Jesus' twelve disciples began following him, they had full lives: jobs, families, commitments, daily schedules, homes. When Jesus called them to be his closest followers, he called them away from every bit of that. They left everything they knew, and for three years straight, they focused on following him. They basically cut off the other ties in their lives, in order to listen to him, their rabbi.

At that time, there was a saying that a disciple should walk so closely to his rabbi that the dust kicked up by him could be found on the disciple's sandals. That's what Jesus' followers tried to do.

We often get the impression that the disciples didn't actually know Jesus all that well when we read Bible stories about them. They don't seem to understand much of what Jesus is talking about. Instead, they seem confused and bewildered. They make lots of blunders and mistakes. They perpetually ask questions.

But they keep following. They let Jesus' voice be the biggest noise in their lives, and they let his dust keep falling on their sandals. It takes time to know someone, and the disciples are giving whatever time it takes.

In the last days of Jesus' ministry on earth, the disciples still seem mixed up about him—some a little, one a lot. In the garden of Gethsemane, Judas betrays Jesus to the religious leaders of the day, handing the Lord over to be killed. Peter later tries to fight the men arresting Jesus— apparently he doesn't understand that Jesus came into the world to die. And Thomas, after Jesus dies and rises from the dead three days later, doubts that the man standing in front of him is actually Jesus.

But at some point, Jesus' message finally clicks with these men. After following Jesus around for three years, having cast aside the rest of their lives in order to listen to him, they *get* it. When Jesus ascends to heaven to be with his Father again, the disciples (including, not long after, Judas's replacement) are ready to be entrusted with the ministry Jesus began.

With the help of the Holy Spirit, Jesus' disciples then bring the good news of God's redemption to the far corners of their world. Often this puts them in great danger, and church tradition tells us that several disciples are so confident of who Jesus is that they're willing to be killed for their belief in him. They follow him faithfully, even to their deaths.

Why do they do this? Because their rabbi's message has sunk deeply into their hearts. They have made him the most important thing—so important that everything else in life could come to a total standstill.

What can we learn from this? It's simple. God has astonishing things to teach us about himself, just like Jesus taught his disciples. When we begin to *get* who God is, we'll change for the better. We'll have less confusion and fewer questions. We'll have weaker doubts. We'll find confidence in our Savior. We'll develop faith that just might be unshakable.

But as with the disciples, most of the things God has to teach us will take time to sink in. They take discipline and focus. And most of the time that means stillness: putting everything else to rest for a while, in order to rest in Jesus.

The question is, are we willing?

A beautiful heart rests in stillness
to hear God's voice clearly.

Discussion Starters

1. One of the Ten Commandments that God gives his people is that they should "remember to observe the Sabbath"[33] and rest from their work one day a week. Do you remember the Sabbath in your life? If not, how do you think things might change if you did?

2. How long did it take for the disciples to begin understanding who Jesus was and what his ministry was about? How can that be encouraging to us? How can that challenge us in the ways we follow Jesus today?

3. What's some of the noise that tends to grab your attention? How does it keep you from listening for God and spending time with only him?

God knows that we need his love far more than we need rules.

14

A *Heart* That Celebrates

Over the Wall:
An Elimination Story

Something Anna was eating was making her sick. That was the part that was easy to figure out. The harder part was determining what, of all the foods a person can eat and of all the ingredients in those foods, was making her sick. Even harder than that was having to say no to certain foods that had become her dietary staples.

Anna and I were roommates, so I had a front-row seat and a cheerleader role in her effort to start feeling well. The process started when Anna noticed that her stomach would get distended occasionally and that at other times she would feel either ill or oddly low on energy. She had a hunch that these health swings were connected to what she was eating, so she began eliminating food types, one at a time, to see whether that might help.

She tried going gluten-free, she tried going dairy-free, she tried going sugar-free, she tried going caffeine-free,

and so on. With certain eliminations, she saw clear improvement in how her body reacted. On one hand, that was great news, but on the other hand, it was a hard pill to swallow.

"Now I just have to have self-control to not eat those things," Anna said to me one day. She was stating the obvious, not so much because it needed stating but because, in this case, "the obvious" would be really difficult to do.

Ask anyone who has ever tried to cut out foods they enjoy, and they'll tell you it can be brutally difficult. We develop tastes for things, and when we're used to having something we like, we don't easily swipe that food out of our meal plans. But when something you enjoy is making you sick, getting rid of the sickness is worth the temporary pain of missing what you enjoy. I went through an elimination phase similar to Anna's when I was in college, also for health reasons, and I had a tough time getting through mine too. I felt better in the end, and I was healthier, but it took a while before I stopped wanting to eat the things that I knew weren't good for me.

One big trick to success in the healthy-digestion process, I had found, was looking ahead. Anna discovered this too. I would focus on the end result, reminding myself how out-of-sorts my stomach felt after eating certain things. I would focus on that *before* letting myself have any of those things. And I would think about how healthy and energized I would feel after eating the things that didn't have negative effects—I'd let those thoughts become my motivation to grab what was good.

Having been through an elimination of my own, it was neat for me to be able to encourage Anna in hers. I felt like I had a unique view on something: Not only had I seen the hard process, but I had also seen the rewards. Whenever she felt like she might be up against a wall, I could look over from the other side and tell her from experience, "It's really worth it, even if you can't see that now. Do what's good for you—you'll be so glad you did."

Do what's good for you—you'll be so glad you did. When you care about someone and you know from experience what you're talking about, that's the kind of message that can be beyond easy to share. You want what's best for them! You want to see them get through the struggle and find the joy at the end!

However, when you're the person who feels up against a wall or pulled in the wrong direction, *Do what's good for you* is the kind of message that can be beyond difficult to hear. Because how can you know if what's being described as good, really is good? What's actually good doesn't always seem good in the moment.

Of course, not only is this true in a discussion of food and nutrition, but it also extends way beyond those things.

The Rules Come Second

Generally speaking, there are two reasons why one person might take advice from another person. The first reason is *authority/expertise*. If we trust that another person is more knowledgeable and more experienced at something than we are, we're more likely to prize their perspective on that thing.

If you wanted to learn how to become a hairstylist, you probably wouldn't ask an investment banker for all the best industry tips. And vice versa. You seek knowledge and wisdom from those who have it. That's why, when Anna was eliminating foods from her diet, even though I wasn't an expert at that, she valued my thoughts and observations along with her other research. She knew I had some experience to offer.

The second reason people take advice is based on *connection/care*. The people who are connected with you and care about you will often have useful insights that apply specifically to you. If you're studying to become a surgeon, but your best friends know that every day you dream of being an illustrator, those friends might suggest that you put down the training scalpels in favor of some drawing pencils. In this example, your friends might know absolutely nothing about the world of art, but they know *you*, which makes their thoughts distinctly beneficial too.

But the point of this chapter is not what your friends have to say about your career or passions, and it's not what a financial officer thinks about your current haircut. The point here is what God has to say about your daily life and the decisions you make in it. Every single decision, ever.

Sometimes we make our choices as if God either doesn't know what he's talking about or doesn't care at all about our well-being. What I mean is this: We read the Bible, and although we can see clearly what it says about certain things, we do different things instead. There's an abundance of easy examples of this: gossiping, lying, disrespecting parents, having sex outside of marriage, being greedy, misusing God's name, failing to care about God's church, failing to care for God's world. Each of these actions, in its own particular way, is awful for us. And in the end, not one of them is a source of joy. We will *not* be glad we did them.

To understand better why these actions don't lead to joy, it's helpful to take a look at how God gives laws and

rules. He has a captivating pattern in the Bible, and it's worth keeping in mind when we approach our choices, no matter if they're big or small.

The pattern starts at the very beginning, in Genesis 1. God creates a world full of life and provision, capping it off by making man and woman in his very own image. God also gives the people everything they could need or want: food to eat, a glorious place to live in, good work to do, and a walking-in-the-garden-together relationship with God himself. It's not until after God supplies everything they need and gives them access to himself that he gives a command. He tells them, "Be fruitful and multiply. Fill the earth and govern it. Reign over the fish in the sea, the birds in the sky, and all the animals that scurry along the ground."[34]

Just a few chapters later, in the midst of a world gone wrong, where "everything [humans] thought or imagined was consistently and totally evil,"[35] God provides again. Rather than destroy everyone and everything, he rescues the humanity he has created and loves. He chooses the one faithful man, Noah, and spares both him and his family from a worldwide flood. And again, it's *after* God has supplied for them so miraculously that he gives this family commands about their lifestyle: "Be fruitful and multiply. Fill the earth."[36]

Later, with Abraham, God promises to make him great and to give him descendants as numerous as the stars. God promises to be faithful to him and to provide land for his family's livelihood. And *then* he tells Abraham to take the sign of his covenant, circumcision.[37]

Years later, after Abraham's descendants have become an entire nation of people, God leads them out of Egypt, protecting them and feeding them continually, day and night. He brings them to Mount Sinai, and he promises that he will make them his "special treasure from among all the peoples on earth."[38] *Then* he gives them the Ten Commandments.

Each of these stories highlights a monumental, life-altering moment in the history of God's people. And in each story, the pattern is unmistakable: God gives and protects and loves and promises first. He doesn't direct his people how to live until later.

Why does God work like this? Well, he created people. As the creator of all humans, he's the one true expert on humanity.

God knows that because of our sinfulness, we need restrictions and rules. He knows that on our own, we are not wise enough to choose what's best for ourselves. But God also knows that we need his love far more than we need rules. He knows we need to be connected and cared for. The rules won't save us; they can't, no matter how well we obey them. God's love, on the other hand, is total rescue.

The crazy catch, though, is that when we have experienced God's rescue—being loved and accepted and forgiven, despite the fact that our sinful hearts deserve to be cast aside, rejected, and forgotten—we will *want* to obey God's rules. We will be so moved by his deep expression of love that we won't be able to help making one of our own: obedience. Even if we don't fully understand God's commands in the moment, we will trust his love and believe that his vantage point on them is better than ours. And we'll obey.

Obedience is a celebration. It's gratitude that we have a God who sees beyond the walls that frustrate or confuse

us. It's gladness, looking to the future and believing that what God offers—including first his love and also his commands for living—is best for us. It's joy, giving whatever we can to the One who has already given us everything.

> *A beautiful heart celebrates God's commands because it trusts in his love, which comes first.*

Discussion Starters

1. How do you look at the topic of obedience? Do you view it as a celebration, or are you more likely to think of it as a nuisance or a chore? What does that suggest about how you view God?

2. What does God's pattern of "love first, command later" tell us about him? Does that change how you think about his commands? If so, how?

3. What's one area of obedience that you struggle with? Do you think your struggle has something to do with doubting God's right to have authority? Does it have something to do with you doubting God's care? How do you think you might discover joy in this area of obedience?

Live

IN A WAY THAT GIVES OTHERS

the best

possible picture

of what it means to

BeLong

to God

15

A *Heart* That Chooses

Making Other Plans:
A Lake House Story

When it comes to spending time with certain people, sometimes you know you can't. You can't because you shouldn't. Spending time with Jake and Wyatt was pretty much an even split: half the time I could and did, but half the time I knew I shouldn't so I wouldn't.

I knew Jake and Wyatt from school. They were nice guys, fun to be around, and easy to talk with. We were friends. I liked them and enjoyed hanging out with them between classes and on campus.

But.

Both Jake's and Wyatt's families liked to get away at the same lake that our family did. It's a place called Cedar Creek Lake, located about an hour outside of Dallas. The lake is huge, and it has homes, cottages, and campsites all around the shoreline. Plenty of people either own or rent little spots at Cedar Creek so they can spend time on

the water during weekends or while on vacation. Our family had a place on the lake that we went to regularly, and Jake's and Wyatt's families did too.

Brittany and I had a great time at the lake. We'd go tubing or waterskiing, swim near the shore, and have conversations under the sun. It was good, innocent fun—but that wasn't the only kind of activity available at Cedar Creek Lake. We knew, because Jake and Wyatt invited us to join them at lake house parties fairly often.

Based on the conversations I had had with Jake and Wyatt at school, I had a pretty good idea of what their lake house parties might look like. They'd meet up with some friends at a house somewhere. They'd be sure that no adults were around and that the alcohol was flowing freely. Maybe people would be smoking pot or hooking up. They had mentioned these kinds of things to me before, never in a "hush, hush" way. To them, this behavior seemed almost normal.

"Do you girls want to come?"

Even though I was friends with Jake and Wyatt, even though I knew we often had fun together, and even though Brittany and I liked having opportunities to talk with them about what we believe, for us, the parties were still a definite no-go.

We didn't want to surround ourselves with things that didn't match our values and might become temptations. We didn't want to jump into situations where lots of people might pressure us to conform and where almost nobody would encourage us to stay strong. And no matter how normal these guys thought their behavior was, we didn't want to risk giving them the impression that we supported things that were illegal, not to mention dangerous and self-destructive.

So when it came to Jake and Wyatt, 50 percent of the time I was excited to hang out with them: in the hallways at school, around a chemistry lab table, or in the gym during PE. But for the other 50 percent of the time, when they were at the lake and headed to a party, Brittany and I always made sure to have other plans.

To Eat or Not to Eat?

In the years after Jesus' death and resurrection, the early Christian churches had a lot of questions about a lot of things. They were trying to figure out how Christianity was supposed to work, and God hadn't given them an enormous manual for that. He had instead given them a person, a Savior. So they were looking at Jesus' life and his teachings, and based on those, they were working to figure out what it meant to live as people of faith.

But Jesus' life and teachings didn't always explain everything in precise detail. Jesus had explained everything that ultimately matters, but he hadn't made a list of all the dos and don'ts for all eternity. So people had questions. We find one example of this in 1 Corinthians 10, where a church in a place called Corinth seems to have asked the apostle Paul, the writer of 1 Corinthians, some particular questions about food.

We can tell from reading this passage that apparently in Corinth there was a pagan ritual where people dedicated food to their idols before eating it. We can also tell that the ritual seems to have put Corinthian Christians in an awkward position: Should they eat the food dedicated to idols, or should they keep away from it totally? And if they aren't sure whether their food has been dedicated to an idol, should they always check before eating?

What's interesting about Paul's response to the Corinthians is that most of his answer isn't specifically about their questions. Instead, he backs up and looks at the issue from a much broader perspective. He addresses their particular concerns, but he seems to be saying that there's a much bigger issue here. In other words, the people are asking, *Are we allowed to eat meat that has been sacrificed to idols?* and Paul is saying, *What's important here isn't what's happening with your digestive system. It's what's in your heart that matters.*

Paul makes this point by reminding the Corinthians about the time when God was leading his people toward the Promised Land. Paul writes that those people had the right "food," a spiritual food: They were being guided by God's presence every single day. Yet they dishonored God, Paul says, by craving evil things and by celebrating in "pagan revelry."[39] They were sexually immoral too, and they grumbled against God, even though he was providing faithfully for them.[40] Although their food was perfect, the fruit of their lives was terrible.

From there, Paul gets into the specifics. He tells the Corinthians three things:

- they can eat food from the marketplace. (verses 25-26)
- sometimes they can eat food others give them. (verse 27)
- sometimes they can't eat food others give them. (verse 28)

But these three rules and permissions aren't the point of what Paul is saying. We know that because each of them has either a *because* or an *if* attached to it.

Paul says that the Corinthian Christians can eat marketplace food *because* everything on earth belongs to God. In other words, the food at the marketplace is God's, not an idol's, no matter who in Corinth might say or think otherwise. Paul also tells the Christians that they can eat food given to them by others—that is, *if* they haven't been told that the food was sacrificed to an idol. The "if" makes a difference, Paul says, because if a Christian knowingly eats—in the presence of someone else—food sacrificed to an idol, that other person could be given the wrong idea about Christianity. They could get the impression that the Christians' God can be worshiped along with other gods, which he absolutely can't.[41]

Okay. Now the question is, what does this have to do with us?

It's a safe bet that none of us is dealing with idol-food questions like this New Testament church was. But we have our own issues and our own pressing questions, don't we?

> What should I do to know God better?
>
> How can I learn to show more respect to my parents?
>
> Is it a good idea for me to participate in this activity, or not?
>
> Is it appropriate for me to wear this outfit, or not?
>
> Should I keep listening to this music, or should I choose something else?
>
> How much time should I be spending with these friends?
>
> How should I respond to this person I've had a conflict with?

What boundaries should I have in this relationship?

Am I giving my best to my work/activities?

How much should I get involved in at church/youth group?

And so on.

If we look carefully here, we'll see that this passage can have a *lot* to do with us. It can have a lot to do with our questions today, and it can teach us plenty.

Take note: Never in this passage does Paul tell the Corinthians to do good things because doing good things is the most important thing, and never does he say they should do good things in order to be good in God's sight. No, he takes the focus off their *doing* and instead points toward *beings*: God and others.

The Corinthians' original question was, "What can we eat?" Paul's answer to that question had two parts. First: *Remember that everything is God's.* Second: *Live in a way that gives others the best possible picture of what it means to belong to God.*

Whatever our questions about behavior might be today, the answers are still the same: Doing good is not the point. Everything belongs to God. Live to give the best picture of God's love.

You, your family, your friends, your body, your time, your money, your activities, your habits, your commitments—all of it is rightfully God's. And everyone needs to know this God and his perfect love: your family, your friends, your classmates, your coworkers, your teachers, your coaches, your neighbors, the people you want to impress, the people you want to ignore, the people you wish you could forget about. Your life is to be a taste of God's goodness and

mercy in theirs. It's the best gift you could give anyone, and after knowing and loving God yourself, it's the most important thing you can do.

When you have a choice to make about a behavior, ask yourself: *Would this choice give glory to God?* (Would it honor his authority, obey his Word, highlight his goodness, reflect his selfless love? Or would it be rebellious, stubborn, angry, selfish?) And ask yourself: *Would this behavior give others the best picture of what it means to belong to God?* (Would it show people a life of joy, confidence, generosity, gratitude, humility, courage, patience, trust, peace, dependence, and fullness? Or would it instead look like misery, insecurity, greed, self-centeredness, vanity, worry, dread, fear, dismay, self-reliance, and emptiness?)

If we're looking for wisdom about whether we should or shouldn't do something, our first step should be to stop focusing so much on that particular something. We need to begin with the questions that matter, and those questions are focused on God and his glory. Then, if it's clear that something honors God and points others toward him, we'll have a deep and lasting confidence in choosing that behavior. If something dishonors God or confuses others about him, we won't. And we'll understand why we shouldn't choose it.

A beautiful heart chooses actions that
glorify God and give others the best picture
of what it means to belong to God.

Discussion Starters

1. When the Corinthians ask Paul about food, what is his response? What can we learn from his reply?

2. What is one behavior in your life that you're not sure is right or wrong? How much have you thought about whether it's right or wrong?

3. With that one behavior in mind, ask yourself the questions in the paragraph that begins with "When you have a choice to make" on the previous page. What becomes clear after asking these questions? How do you think you should respond? (If you're still not sure, ask a trusted Christian friend or mentor to help you think through these questions.)

Part Four

Your Heart for Others

No other approval
could ever add to
what's already ours
in Christ.

16

A *Heart* That Gets Vulnerable

Not Her Best Foot Forward:
A New Girl Story

In fashion, people call it "playing up your best features." If there's a part of your body that you don't particularly appreciate, style gurus can recommend all kinds of clothing and styling tricks for hiding it. The last thing you'd want to do, they say, is emphasize a "problem area."

But the point of this chapter isn't what "they" or anybody else says about dressing for your body type, because we're not really talking about fashion here. Most of us don't need tips for playing up our best features anyway. We already do it in all of life, all the time. We are experts at hiding "flaws" and showcasing our strengths.

For example, Lucy talks endlessly about drama club (she's got a starring role), but she avoids mentioning friendships, because most of hers are faltering. Or Joanna goes on and on about how sweet her baby sister is, but you won't hear her say anything about her parents, whose marriage is splintering. Or Rachelle spends all her time in her school's gym, where her athletic records are lifted high on the wall, but she goes home only when she has to, because she's embarrassed by her neighborhood. Or Brenda broadcasts grand plans for her future, but she doesn't speak about the massive hurts from her past.

In our own unique ways, each of us does it. We march out into the world, wearing our most polished image and our most sparkling profile. We live in an airbrushed and photo-edited world, after all. Nearly everything our culture values seems to imply that we should never show anything but our gleaming side. But all this gloss has also brought out endless irony, because if all we ever do is display our best behavior, we miss out on prime opportunities to really *become* our best.

Here's what I mean. My friend Tiffany has had more first-impression moments than most teenagers ever will. She had gone to seven different schools by the time she graduated high school: three elementary schools, one middle school, and three high schools. Her dad's job required their family to move around quite a bit, and sometimes getting settled into a different place meant trying out one school for a while, then deciding to find a better fit.

Despite moving around as much as she did, over the years Tiffany found acceptance and belonging in a number of really good friendships. In fact, her friendships are deeper than many I've seen. But there's a twist to her story, because Tiffany formed relationships by doing what's practically the opposite of putting her best foot forward: Tiffany got vulnerable, *fast*.

Faced with a new place and new people, not to mention

all the insecurity and awkwardness that can come along with that kind of situation, Tiffany would simply take the risk to be uncomfortable. She'd try out a Bible study where she didn't know anybody, she'd serve with a church she'd been part of for just a couple of weeks, and she'd introduce herself to someone who seemed to have similar interests. She'd share some personal details with someone who didn't know her very well yet. She'd admit to struggling with some particular issue. She'd scrub off some of the gloss, in other words. She'd let herself feel uncomfortable, and she'd remind herself that it's okay for people to see some of the grit that helps make her who she is.

Most of the time when Tiffany did this, she felt at least a little uncomfortable and out on a limb. It was a risk, getting vulnerable with people she didn't know. Would they accept her? Be indifferent to her? Reject her? After opening up her life—not just a pristine image, but her real, often messy life—to someone new, would they slam the door in her face?

Despite hard questions and realistic concerns like these, Tiffany kept getting vulnerable. She made a consistent effort to let people see her in confident places and in less-than-confident ones too. Showing both those sides of herself simply felt *right*.

Because it was. It is.

The Tax Collector? Really?

In Luke 18, Jesus tells a parable about two men on their way to the Temple. The primary point of this parable is about how these two men approached God differently. But there's another point that's demonstrated too, and that one becomes clear when we shine a spotlight on just one of the men, a tax collector.

Back in Jesus' time, it was well known that most tax collectors had a habit of collecting much more than just taxes. Many of them, in fact, became rich by charging extra "fees" and skimming off the top of their collection pot. These greedy ways, combined with the fact that they worked hand-in-hand with Gentiles, made tax collectors some of the most despised and looked-down-upon people in all of Israel. They were seen as absolute traitors and total cheats.

But Jesus gives us a different picture when he tells of a tax collector in the Temple:

> *The tax collector stood at a distance and dared not even lift his eyes to heaven as he prayed. Instead, he beat his chest in sorrow, saying, "O God, be merciful to me, for I am a sinner."*[42]

Now, most of the people listening to Jesus' story probably wouldn't have been shocked at this. Obviously the tax collector was a sinner. He was one of the worst people around, in their minds. He didn't deserve to look upward at God, they might've thought. They might've hoped that all his chest thumpings *hurt*.

But if that's all they thought, their perspective was apparently way off course, because Jesus is presenting this tax collector as the good guy in the story. He's someone who is made right in God's eyes. In Luke 18:14 Jesus says, "I tell you, this sinner . . . returned home justified before God." For all his treacherous, cheating ways, the tax collector is somehow getting something important right. That gives us every reason to give him a closer look.

What's good about the tax collector? I think it's something that's both simple and fiercely compelling. It's what

turns him into a pile of vulnerability, smack in the middle of the Temple court. It's what makes him so vulnerable that he doesn't even seem to realize it.

This man knows the ugliness of his sin. He really, really knows it. His entire prayer is a confession. He doesn't claim to bring God anything but a sinful self. What he wants desperately—eyes downcast, standing at a distance, pounding his chest over it—is God's mercy.

Let's remember that this man is praying at a public site, in perfect view of everyone. His words are loud enough to be heard, and his grief over his sin is plain enough to be easily observed. You might even say that by beating his chest, he's making a bit of a scene. But he doesn't seem to care how those around him might respond, and apparently it doesn't bother him that others might hear his confession. He is being his real, sinful self before God, admitting the thing that shames him most deeply. With anyone and everyone watching.

Do you see what's happening here? Because this tax collector has his eyes trained on the Lord and on forgiveness, he also oozes vulnerability in the eyes of others.

It's an amazing thing, and it's exactly what should happen in any story of God's mercy.

When we repent before God and experience his forgiveness, we stand before perfection wearing our most wretched rags. No carefully crafted image could make any difference, and playing up our best features won't change anything either. God sees the ugliest corners of our hearts—and he loves us. Not only does the strength of God's love give us access to him (the most important thing!), it also accomplishes other changes in us. For starters, it makes us more comfortable with being vulnerable.

If we, as sinful people, can be accepted by the perfect God, then we have all the acceptance anyone could ever need. No other approval could ever add to what's already ours. And no rejection on earth could take away from it. That's why we can stand before others honestly too: in all our awkwardness, insecurity, neediness, weakness, and yes, even our sinfulness. We don't have anything to hide. We can toss out all concerns about our image when we're focused on the God who was willing to give us his.

And you know what? We'll probably find *more* acceptance from others when we're not worried about how they'll react after seeing who we really are. Like my friend Tiffany found, we'll likely discover that it's easier to get close to people when we're not constantly hiding our fallenness from them. That's typically how things work: When we do the things that glorify God and celebrate his goodness—such as admitting our shortcomings and celebrating his grace—*we* are more fulfilled too.

It's no wonder. Since God is the only true goodness in us, more of him in us is how things get better.

> *A beautiful heart gets vulnerable, being*
> *honest about its need for God's mercy.*

Discussion Starters

1. What's the connection between forgiveness from God and vulnerability with other people? How do we see that in Jesus' story of the tax collector?

2. What's a weakness in you that you have a hard time letting others see? In what ways is it difficult for you to be vulnerable with people?

3. How should remembering God's forgiveness help you be more vulnerable with others? What's one way that you can practice that this week?

More of you, Lord. More of your heart in mine.

17

A *Heart* That Is Wise

Seeing Patterns:
A Naive-Me Story

When I was a teenager, there were plenty of times when I would've much rather spent my time with guys around than with just girls. I loved all my friends, girls and guys, but the guys in particular were always uncomplicated and to the point, never any drama involved. And it often seemed that with some guys thrown into the mix, the girls were more likely to be drama-free too. So I almost always preferred a coed group.

One of the things my friends and I did in high school was to assemble a group of guys and girls and play touch football together after school. Texas is full of lifetime football fans, so most of us had grown up loving the sport. That's why, when the weather warmed up, we'd get an itch for running routes and throwing passes, and

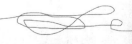

somehow a plan for a game would spontaneously happen. It wasn't anything fancy, just a quick game on a field next to the school parking lot, but I couldn't get enough. I was having carefree fun in the fresh air with friends I cared about.

But that's exactly the kind of situation where I was at risk for getting myself into trouble without even realizing it. I have this thing, you see, about guys and boundaries because I'm so comfortable with them. It's basically a blind spot; I wouldn't even know about it, if not for the other people in my life who care about me enough to make me aware of it. My brother-in-law has been one of those people. Just the other day, in fact, Shaun was dishing out some good-natured teasing, talking about me to a friend of ours while I was standing right there.

"Lauren would say, '*Heeeey*, Brian! How *are* you!?' and be touching the guy's shoulder, and then later she'd say to me, 'Why is Brian—why is he asking me out? Why does he want my number? I don't like him like that at all!'"

What I've had to learn is that the answer to those *whys* is right there in the story: because I was talking to a guy in a way that probably made it seem like I might be interested in him, and because at the same time I was touching his upper arm.

Another thing I've been known to do is to accept a date (or nearly accept one) without realizing that I'm being asked on a date. A guy has said, "Hey, do you want to go to dinner or coffee sometime?" and I've responded in an instant—"Oh! That would be so *fun!*"

When the words came out of my mouth, what I was thinking was exactly what I said: That would be fun. *This is a good friend, and I know I would have a good time with*

him. But to be fair, I can see now that based on the circumstances, that's probably not what I communicated. Instead of *That would be fun,* chances are the guy heard me say, *Yes! I want to go out with you!*

As I began learning this about myself, I had to circle back to a guy or two to make sure I was being clear about myself. Once, while dating one guy, I agreed to go to coffee with another guy friend. It wasn't until after I had said, "Sure, let's meet up!" that I put two and two together and realized the friend seemed to be pursuing something more than just friendship. Thankfully, by that time I had also realized that the week of our scheduled meet-up was way too crammed for coffee.

I e-mailed and apologized for having to cancel, explaining that my boyfriend and I had promised to help prepare for a friend's birthday party that week and that I'd be more busy than I had previously thought. While sending the e-mail, I prayed that if my suspicion about this friend's motive was right, he wouldn't be hurt or feel that I had led him on. I definitely hadn't intended for either to happen. In the end, he was gracious: "It sounds like you're really happy, and I'm happy for you."

Whether my hunch about him was on-target, I might never know for sure. Either way, though, I was grateful to catch myself in my naive tendencies for a change. Although I've never been a person who dates a lot (no matter how this chapter might make it seem), I still had a clear pattern of potentially confusing the guys around me, and I didn't want to keep that going. It was good to curb those behaviors. I could see that without learning new ways to interact, I would risk damaging my relationships and snubbing my friends, while barely noticing it.

Love, Faithfulness, and a Bumbling Idiot

What would you ask for if God appeared to you suddenly and told you he would give you anything? It's a scenario that almost feels straight out of a genie bottle, I know, but in 1 Kings 3 we see a man who was actually faced with that question.

The man in the story is King Solomon, David and Bathsheba's son. When we meet him in this chapter, he has taken over the rule of Israel from his father, and we can see that he's doing pretty well at it. The first few verses tell us that Solomon loves God, that he's working to complete a Temple where God's people can worship, and that he's seeking to protect the Israelites by building a wall around their city. We know he's not perfectly obedient (he has married a non-Jewish woman, which was forbidden by God's law at that time), but his love for God is clearly what drives him. An obvious example of this is that he goes to the most prominent altar in Israel and sacrifices one thousand offerings to God there.

Think about that: one thousand offerings!

The night of all those sacrifices, God comes to Solomon in a dream. His message is simple: "What do you want? Ask, and I will give it to you!"[43]

The universe is at Solomon's fingertips. God has left *everything* open to him. And Solomon's request is extremely telling. He doesn't take a moment to ponder what the most extravagant request might be. He doesn't turn ridiculous and ask for endless wishes. No. The first thing Solomon does is offer God humility and praise:

> Solomon replied, "You showed great and faithful love to
> your servant my father, David, because he was honest

*and true and faithful to you. And you have continued to
show this great and faithful love to him today by giving
him a son to sit on his throne.*

*"Now, O LORD my God, you have made me king
instead of my father, David, but I am like a little child
who doesn't know his way around. And here I am in the
midst of your own chosen people, a nation so great and
numerous they cannot be counted!"*[44]

I am like a little child who doesn't know his way around.
Did you catch that? It's a sentence that's also a clue to
Solomon's mind-set, telling us that he views God as great
and himself as small. We might even say that, standing before God's goodness, remembering God's love and faithfulness to his family, Solomon feels a bit like a bumbling idiot.

With that in mind, what the king says next makes perfect sense:

*"Give me an understanding heart so that I can govern
your people well and know the difference between right
and wrong. For who by himself is able to govern this great
people of yours?"*[45]

Even in making his request, what Solomon seeks for
himself is actually for others and for God's glory. He's asking for the ability to lead God's people well, admitting that he
can't do it by himself. He's saying that he values knowing the
difference between right and wrong, because that's what's
necessary for governing well, and because on his own he
doesn't know how. He's repeatedly recognizing that his
leadership of Israel isn't really his at all: *"your* people," he
tells the Lord—*"your* own chosen people," "this great people
of *yours."*

Look at Solomon's request again. What Solomon is asking for is this: *More of you, Lord. More of your heart in mine.*

If statistics mean anything, then most of us won't ever be royalty, rule a nation, or have God visit us personally in a dream. But every one of us can learn something valuable from Solomon's humble request in 1 Kings 3. Every one of us has the same core problem that Solomon did: blind spots. We struggle to know what's right, we need God's heart to take over ours, and without God's help we become possible hazards to everyone around us. Sometimes we're so blind that we don't even see the destructive patterns we're repeating.

More of him. We need more of God's heart at the center of us. The 1 Kings 3 passage calls that *wisdom*—like Solomon, we would be wise to want it above anything.

A beautiful heart relies on God's wisdom to
reveal destructive patterns and blind spots.

Discussion Starters

1. If you could ask God for one thing, would it really be wisdom? Why or why not? What does that suggest about how you feel about God and about yourself? (In answering these questions, it might help to compare your responses to Solomon's.)

2. What might your friends and family say is a destructive behavior pattern in your life? What makes it destructive? In what ways does it show an absence of wisdom?

3. Read James 1:5. What would be the first thing that would change about you if you had an understanding heart, one that knows the difference between right and wrong? Are you willing to ask God for that? Why or why not?

SERVE ONE ANOTHER IN ♥ LOVE

GALATIANS 5: 13

18

A *Heart* That Serves

Seizing His Opportunity:
A Fame Story

"**I** really think you should do this," Scott told me, nodding earnestly.

I looked at him and nodded right back. "You know," I said, "I think maybe you're right."

It was two months after my accident. My family and I had already seen God use our still-unfolding story in astounding ways. In the earliest days of my healing, several major magazines and news outlets had taken interest in what was happening with me and had arranged interviews with my parents for updates. Even when outcomes for my recovery were extremely uncertain, whenever my mom and dad were asked about me, they always took the opportunity to share about our family's trust in God. They believed, all the way through, that God is good and loving and in control, and they said that whenever anybody asked them about me.

143

As a result, people from all over the country and even around the world had heard a fresh telling of God's faithfulness and goodness. Even though the healing process was difficult and taxing for all of us, we were honored that it had become a platform we could use to talk boldly about God and to give him glory. That said, we also knew that because of my needs during recovery, some potential uses of our new platform absolutely could not be options. Which, unfortunately, is where this story with Scott came into the picture.

Scott and I had known each other for several years and had even worked with each other at one point. He had heard through mutual friends that some producers had contacted me to offer me a spot on a televised dancing competition. Almost immediately after finding out about that, he had called me up and asked if I wanted to talk about the offer with anyone. I told him that sounded great—I had actually just been praying that morning about how I should respond, and I liked the thought of tossing around the idea with somebody.

But there's one detail I haven't mentioned yet: I was still *heavily* dosed with nerve-pain medication at that point. The accident had happened only two months earlier, and although I was making progress, I had a long way to go. My doctors had prescribed rest and carefully managed physical therapy, and they had strongly advised against certain kinds of activity—in particular, anything where I might risk hitting my head and further injuring my still-healing brain. My neurologist (brain doctor) had told me that if I were to hit my head against anything hard at that point, it could cause a second trauma worse than the first. In a situation like that, I might never recover.

It hadn't occurred to me, in my medicated state, that being lifted and spun around on a dance floor all day for weeks on end might be just the sort of activity where a novice dancer could hit her head. So after talking with Scott, I approached my family and told them I was considering signing on to the competition.

"Lo," they said, "now probably isn't the best time." And they kindly reminded me of why I needed to take it easy.

So I reconvened with Scott to let him know where things stood. "The risk of hitting my head is the main reason why I can't do it," I told him.

"I think you should call your doctor and double-check."

I tried to explain that calling the doctor wouldn't change anything. "I already know that I need to be cautious for more than just two months."

But Scott wasn't convinced. Later, in fact, he had a conversation with my parents over the phone where he tried to persuade *them* to let me sign on. When they firmly turned down the idea and again expressed why rest was necessary, Scott became insistent. They still wouldn't budge, though, at which point Scott became furious and unhinged. He spewed a stream of alarmingly inappropriate language at my dad and then promptly hung up on him.

It wasn't until after that blowup that we realized Scott had ulterior motives about my potential dancing gig. I had known for a long time that he wanted to be involved in the entertainment industry—TV, movies, etc.—to become *known*. As details came to light, it became clear that Scott had latched on to the idea that this opportunity could somehow make me a star. More than that, though, he had decided that if he could somehow make himself my manager, then he'd have an easy door into showbiz. He had built up this dream in his head until it practically consumed him. In the end, he lost control of his emotions, lost sight of other people, and lost his grip on common sense. All in hopes to wrap himself up in fame.

I don't like telling this story, partly because it was a hurtful experience and partly because I don't like painting a friend in an unflattering light. But a story like this is worth mentioning, because sometimes it's the ugliest stories that can most clearly help us appreciate real beauty.

Our Filthy Example to Follow

The problem with Scott is that he's just like pretty much everybody else: me, you, my friends, your friends, all of us. We're incredibly adept at caring for ourselves and not so great at caring for others. We put our own needs and wants first, and *maybe* after that we'll squeeze in some attention for others. Maybe.

But part of what God's love shows us is that when we do that, we have things backward.

On the last evening before Jesus was arrested and later crucified, he taught his disciples an important lesson. The whole group had gathered in a room together to celebrate the Jewish holiday Passover, which centers on a particular meal. But before any group ate a meal together, it was customary that each of them would have their feet washed.

This was a filthy job. In that day, people traveled primarily by foot, wearing sandals, and most of the roads they walked on had been formed out of dirt. Also traveling on those roads were animals carrying burdens or towing loads, which means there were piles of animal droppings all around. If you missed sidestepping even one of those land mines, you'd have a little something extra on your feet that day. Those are the reasons why the task of foot washing was reserved for servants. It was a lowly job.

The book of John tells us what happened, though, when Jesus and his disciples were getting ready to eat:

> *Jesus knew that the Father had given him authority over everything and that he had come from God and would return to God. So he got up from the table, took off his robe, wrapped a towel around his waist, and poured water into a basin. Then he began to wash the disciples' feet, drying them with the towel he had around him.*[46]

Later in the passage, we see that Jesus' willingness to take on this filthy role offends Peter, one of the disciples. Peter tells Jesus, "No, you will never ever wash my feet!"[47]

Jesus' response to Peter is almost forceful: "Unless I wash you, you won't belong to me."[48]

After Jesus finishes washing all those grubby, grimy feet, he sits down and explains to his disciples why he did it. He reminds them why they call him their Teacher and Lord: because that's precisely what he is. Then he tells them that since he, as their Teacher and Lord, has washed their feet, that means that foot washing is both a lesson they should learn from their Teacher and a command they should obey from their Lord. Washing feet is something they should learn and do.

Okay, let's recap for a moment and think about what Jesus is telling his disciples. He's telling them that following him—or as he said to Peter, *belonging* to him—means we don't get to claim any sort of special status. We don't get a place of honor or ease—instead, we get the role of a servant.

We get to be responsible for helping to clean people where they're smeared with the worst kind of sludge.

It sounds gross, unless we remember how disgusting our own feet have been. If we feel clean, it's only because Jesus has come and washed our sin off us. He filled the basin, wrapped the towel around himself, and let all our grime splash onto his own pure skin. Then he carried it to the cross and was killed because of it. And we got to walk away with his spotlessness.

When our hearts are centered on that single truth, we can't help but see that we're lowly. How could we forget such a life-altering gift? How could we try to tell ourselves that we deserve some kind of special status, or that we have the right to walk all over people or look down on them? They're dirty, just as we have been dirty. Whatever grime of sin they wear has the same griminess of whatever sin we've worn ourselves. The sole difference is that we have been washed by the only One who can make us clean.

When our sins have been washed by him, we'll want that same incredible scrub for anyone and everyone else. We'll consider it a privilege to roll up our sleeves and help. We won't hesitate to pick up a bowl and a rag, kneel before someone else, and dip our hands in the dirty water for their sake. It will be a way of sharing and remembering God's goodness.

"I have given you an example to follow," is what Jesus told his disciples that night. "Do as I have done to you."[49]

A beautiful heart follows Jesus' example,
serving in even the lowliest ways and places.

Discussion Starters ♡

1. Why do we tend to care for ourselves before caring for others? What does that say about how much we're thinking about what God has done for us?

2. Can you think of a person you would have a difficult time serving? Why is it hard to imagine serving that person? How should the story of Jesus' sacrifice change how you think about that person?

3. What's one specific way you can follow Jesus' example by serving someone else?

Ask God to help you

faithfully choose him,

so you'll be rooted in the One

who never changes.

19

A *Heart* That Is True

Disappearing Act
in the City:
A Dating Story

I could hardly believe that someone as good-looking as Brooks actually existed. Every single quality I found most physically attractive in a guy, he had. No kidding, every single one. And there he was, day after day, at *my* side. When we walked around the city together, he held my hand, and everyone could see that this gorgeous guy wanted to be with *me*.

It was my "summer of no direction" in New York. I've mentioned before that I didn't have a job or roommates to occupy my time, and I wasn't paying any extra attention to what God might be saying to me either. Instead, I was spending almost all my time with Brooks. Or to more accurately describe it, I was making almost all of my time Brooks's time. I was letting him be the captain of the summer's ship, no question.

Brooks didn't like having deep conversations or being emotionally vulnerable, so whenever we talked, we kept things shallow and on the surface. We'd talk about who we had seen that day, what was going on in New York, or where we might go together later. We'd swap info about our hobbies or our interests, and we'd tell fun stories about our friends. But on the few occasions when, for instance, I tried to discuss his parents' marriage (it was crumbling badly), the conversations didn't go far.

In any other dating relationship or even any other close friendship, I wouldn't have been satisfied by such a shallow connection. I would've wanted and expected to see personal thoughts and feelings shared back and forth regularly, and I would've needed deep, supportive, challenging dialogue to balance out the surface things. But not with Brooks. With Brooks, I was content to walk around neighborhoods, play soccer in parks, visit Central Park with his friends, and go out for dinners—for weeks on end—without really moving beyond chitchat.

On my own and with my friends, I'm not the partying type. I like to grab a good dinner and spend time at great spots around town, but going to a place simply to drink alcohol doesn't make my list of enjoyable evenings. Brooks liked to party, though, and he liked to drink—so what did I do? I went with him.

Thankfully, Brooks never forced me to do things I didn't want to do or didn't feel right doing. He didn't abuse the strong influence he had on me. And while that's one good part of this story, it also helps emphasize just how wrong I was in our relationship: All on my own, I was choosing to give his priorities and interests ultimate weight. I was letting some of my own values and many of my own interests disappear in order to make as much room as possible in my life for his.

But my hopes were still my hopes, and (even though I didn't always behave this way) what was most important to me was still most important to me. That's why I kept telling myself that Brooks had wonderful potential and that someday, if he accepted the Lord, then the two of us could serve God together. Our conversations could be wrapped around what matters, and our activities could serve God and bring him glory. Our shared interests could extend beyond superficial activities with flimsy meaning. We would care about each other's hearts, not just each other's appearances. Brooks would learn how to trust people and be vulnerable. And I could open up too, finally having space to be the real "me" with the guy I liked so much.

The big problem was, though, that I didn't just *like* Brooks. I idolized being with him. That's another way of saying that the reason I was with him wasn't as much because of *him* as it was because of me. I loved how cool it made me feel to be the girl Brooks chose to spend his time with. I let that feeling consume me and drive me, to the point where it upstaged almost everything else.

Brooks's opinion of me became priority number one because I knew if it went downhill, I would lose him. I didn't want to lose him, because losing him would mean losing the feeling I got from being with him. That's why I kept giving him so much sway in our relationship and in what we did together. I needed him to have the best opinion of me, and if I gave him most of the control, I knew his choices for us would show me who he wanted me to be. They would show me which parts of myself I should disregard and which pieces of my life I should push aside in order to keep him.

Little by little, I was letting Brooks's influence change me. I was letting him be the deciding factor in many of my life's choices, and it was decidedly not working.

A Heart Divided

At the end of Luke 10, there is a well-known Bible story about two sisters and Jesus. While traveling through their village, Jesus is invited by Martha into her home. Then it seems she promptly goes to work to show him hospitality by preparing food. Her sister, Mary, on the other hand, sits at Jesus' feet and listens to his teaching.

Martha, sweating it out in the kitchen—just think how long it must've taken to cook a meal back then!—eventually becomes upset that Mary isn't helping. She gripes to Jesus about it, expecting him to tell Mary to get to work, but Jesus doesn't.

> The Lord said to her, "My dear Martha, you are worried and upset over all these details! There is only one thing worth being concerned about. Mary has discovered it, and it will not be taken away from her."[50]

And that's the end of the story. We don't learn how the meal unfolded or whether Martha came out of the kitchen after all. It seems those things aren't important enough to be included in the story. Instead, we see that the key point is this: Martha is doing something wrong, directly in contrast with Mary, who is doing something right.

What about Martha's work in the kitchen is wrong? We can find a hint in one particular word Jesus uses in speaking to her. In the New Testament's original writing, the Greek word used for *worried*—as in, "Martha, you are worried . . . over all these details!"—comes from a root word that suggests division. It gives a picture of something that's split into pieces. In other words, Jesus could've just as easily said, "Martha, you are so *fragmented*!"

With this in mind, the contrast that Jesus brings out between Mary and Martha makes a lot of sense. Mary, he says, has her focus pointed in one clear direction: on him. Martha, on the other hand, has her focus divided into pieces. Although she has welcomed Jesus into her home, now she is committing most of her attention to the kitchen.

Reading a passage like this should turn our eyes inward, toward our own kinds of divided, fragmented focus. That's because, more often than not, we're guilty of being much more like Martha than we are like Mary. We, too, invite Jesus in and then quickly turn our attention elsewhere.

One of the most common examples of this, especially among young women, is the compartmentalizing I did when I was spending time with Brooks. My heart was fragmented between the guy I liked and the God I loved. There was evidence of the division everywhere, because it was impossible for me to be true to one version of myself.

I wanted to have it both ways: to be committed to God and also to be romantically involved with Brooks. But that was impossible, because Brooks's life wasn't devoted to God. That meant my two efforts couldn't overlap. I had to be divided in order to pursue them both. My heart became fragmented, and that was evident in my behavior.

This helps illustrate an important point: It's impossible to be the same person all the time, to be true, when your primary focus is changing back and forth. That's because in any given moment, the thing you're most committed to will steer your thoughts and behavior. If that thing changes with the wind, your behavior will change with the wind too.

You might ask, *What's wrong with behavior that changes back and forth? Can't I be one way with one person or group of people, and another way with another?* Well, on one level you can. We all understand that different types of people and circumstances might bring out different *aspects* of a single personality. The problem comes in when a person's behavior in one scenario is *inconsistent* with her behavior in another scenario.

For example,

- talking about God and the Bible while at church or youth group, but not while at school, at work, or on a team;
- being kind to a certain person only when certain other people aren't around;
- treating a particular behavior as okay when in the company of your friends, but not in the company of your parents or teachers; or
- hiding aspects of your life from others, in general.

What's the problem with these types of actions? That's simple: They're the signals that blare out from an inconsistent heart. Let's remember, after all, that *fragmented* is just another word for *broken*. If your primary focus is split into pieces today, you probably already know that it doesn't work and it doesn't feel good. It doesn't demonstrate that God is always the God of your heart.

Listen, God doesn't need our total devotion. He doesn't need anything; he *is* everything already, no matter what we do with him.

He is *everything*.

God wants us to be true to him, but not because *he* has some need for that. He wants us to be true to him because we need him. We need him to be our everything. In each decision we make and every action we take, we need his direction and influence. Without it, we've already lost ourselves.

Ask God to help you faithfully choose him instead—he'll do it! He'll take the pieces of your life by gathering up the ones that glorify him and chipping away at the ones that don't. What you'll be left with in the end will be consistent, rooted in the One who never changes. Your heart will be dependable, drawing strength from the One who is always there for you. It will find its influence and direction in only one source, the best source.

It will feel every bit as whole as it is.

A beautiful heart is true, faithfully choosing
God's influence and direction.

Discussion Starters

1. In what way(s) are you fragmented and divided? Have you welcomed Jesus into your life, while at the same time giving your primary focus to something or someone else?

2. Have you ever changed yourself or hidden aspects of yourself in a way that doesn't glorify God? In that instance, who was the person or what was the thing you were glorifying instead of glorifying God?

3. How does accepting God's love help us be true in our other relationships? What's one specific way that God's love could help you be true in another relationship today?

20

A *Heart* That Uplifts

Heartache for Good: A Warrior Story

*H*e was probably six or seven, the cutest little guy with dark brown hair, standing with his dad at the hotel elevators. He stood quietly, turned a little toward one side. It was my mom who noticed why.

"Lauren," she whispered, grabbing my elbow, "that little boy doesn't have a hand."

"He doesn't?"

It was difficult to see at first because of the way he was standing. When I looked more closely, I instantly got the sense that this little boy's body positioning was no accident. He kept one arm tucked closely at his side, with that whole side of himself always aimed away from us.

My mom nudged me. "You should go say something to him."

I agreed and took a few steps closer to where he was.

"Hi!" I said.

He looked up at me, his face a little startled. The second he realized I was standing next to him, he readjusted his stance again, to keep that one arm hidden. But he gave me a shy grin. "Hi."

As nonchalantly as possible, I bent at my waist just enough to get a quick look at the arm he was trying to hide. "Hey! I don't have a hand either!" I held out my left arm between us so he could see.

Apparently no other introduction was necessary, because just like that, his floodgates opened, and excitement poured out of him. Suddenly this hunched and hiding little boy was standing confidently and comfortably in front of me. He was smiling broadly and telling me all about why he was staying at this hotel. "I'm going to be a volunteer at the Wounded Warrior race!"

"This is Carter," the boy's dad said with a smile.

The rest of us introduced ourselves and began chatting away while waiting for an elevator. Carter had a lot to say about his special volunteer job that day, and we were all excited to hear about it. My family and I had become pretty familiar with the Wounded Warrior Project since I lost my hand—in fact, the day I met Carter, I was in the middle of training for a WWP event myself. It seemed obvious to me why serving with WWP might mean so much to this little boy.

Wounded Warrior Project is an organization that serves military veterans who have been injured in combat.[51] Many of the veterans who've been wounded in the last decade or so have lost limbs. If you're missing an arm or leg too, volunteering with an organization like WWP— even if you have no affiliation with the military—enables you to serve with a unique sense of camaraderie. It means

a lot to work alongside and benefit others who are facing some of the same struggles you've been facing. It clearly meant a lot to Carter that day. He acted as if he could hardly wait to get started.

As our two families talked and eventually rode an elevator down to the lobby together, I couldn't help but be struck by this little boy and his big, meaningful mission. Based on the way Carter had instinctively hidden his missing hand from view, it was obvious he was dealing with hurts or insecurities about it. Even so, he was finding a way to turn his own struggle around so he could benefit others. And I have no doubt it did.

One thing I've noticed a lot since my accident is that people who've "been there" are uniquely equipped to encourage others who are suffering. A number of my newly close friends are people who've lost limbs, faced recovery, or dealt with trauma themselves. All of them have become highly treasured people in my life.

Why? Because they've walked this road already. They've faced its challenges and its joys. Often they've come up with handy solutions for the bumps that will happen along the way. Other times they simply *get* when things are difficult or when a big milestone should be celebrated. It's such an encouragement to see that there are others who've walked on this same road—even if they're a long way ahead of me on the journey, seeing their footprints helps me feel like they're right here with me. And when times are especially difficult, what you need is someone *right here*. They can give you the strength to keep taking steps in the right direction. They can help you lift your eyes off the struggle long enough to see that even this hard road can lead to someplace remarkable and thrilling.

That's why I love thinking about Carter and his work with wounded veterans. Even though this little boy was still fighting some of the hurts that came with his own missing limb, he wanted to put himself in full view for others who might be struggling on a similar path. Maybe it was awkward or uncomfortable for Carter to have people see his arm that day—based on my interaction with him, I'm guessing it was, at least at first. But he was willing to do it.

What this tells me about Carter is that there is a glimmer of something astonishing in him. This little boy has the willingness to take risks himself, in order to give good to others. It's the kind of thing that halts the breath in your lungs for a moment when you see it. I know it did for me. That's why I'm confident there were plenty of wounded veterans who ran a little faster or smiled a little broader or volunteered a little harder after seeing Carter later that day. What they saw in him—even just a glimmer of it—is enough to change a person profoundly.

Now, think what *more* than a glimmer would do!

Attitude or Action?

Let's be clear: There is only One person who gives the full, astonishing picture. There's only One who risks himself ultimately, in order to give to others.

> He gave up his divine privileges;
>> he took the humble position of a slave
>> and was born as a human being.
> When he appeared in human form,
>> he humbled himself in obedience to God
>> and died a criminal's death on a cross.[52]

That's how the apostle Paul describes Jesus in a letter to the Philippians. But this part of the letter isn't about only Jesus. It's about the Philippians, too. And it's about us. What Paul is doing is explaining what a Christian community should be like:

> *Don't be selfish; don't try to impress others. Be humble, thinking of others as better than yourselves. Don't look out only for your own interests, but take an interest in others, too.*
>
> *You must have the same attitude that Christ Jesus had.*[53]

Do you see that? Paul doesn't tell the Philippians that they should *do* the same things Jesus did. Sure, he advises them about some actions they should take, but when he tells them to be like Jesus, he's talking about what's behind the action: attitude. Thoughts and hearts, the things that drive behavior—these are the parts of ourselves that are supposed to resemble Jesus.

What this means for us is that, like Jesus, we should *want* God's glory. We should want it more than anything else because it should be more important to us than our own status or circumstances. It should be the thing at the center of our thoughts and hearts, the thing that gives us the greatest joy and the best satisfaction. That's an attitude like Jesus had: It seeks out and celebrates God's glory, far above all.

Jesus' defining moment of seeking God's glory was when he took punishment on himself so that others could find God's pardon. He volunteered to be lifted up on a cross, because he knew that action would lift people up, giving them his righteous standing with God. This was

God's glory on display for all to see. But Jesus was God, which means nobody forced him to do it. He wouldn't have died for us if he didn't want to.

While nothing we do could ever come close to matching Jesus' action or attitude, we *can* provide the world with glimmers of it. We can sacrifice our own comfort and convenience in order to show others what God's love looks like. We can crucify our popularity or our schedule or our bank account or our success in order to offer people the attention, time, financial support, and energy they need from us. We can do all those things, not because we simply think we *should* but because God's glorious love in our hearts actually makes us want to.

A beautiful heart wants to sacrifice for
others' good and for God's glory.

Discussion Starters

1. Have you ever seen another person give to others, at a cost to himself or herself? How did that affect you or those who were served?

2. In his letter to the Philippians, what does Paul say church community should look like? Do your relationships with people in your life look like that?

3. How does an attitude like Jesus' impact our actions? How does your attitude lately compare with Jesus'?

21

A *Heart* That Confronts

"You're Going to Call Him": A Breakup Story

*L*ana, a friend of mine, was a church youth leader who took a weekend camping trip with her small group of high school students. The expedition put six young women—Lana plus five soon-to-be high school seniors—together in a camper, on a beach, and around a fire pit from Friday to Sunday. They roasted marshmallows, went for midnight swims, and made several firewood trips. And by the end of the weekend, one of the students, Stephanie, had dumped her boyfriend.

"Prior to this trip, Stephanie was the one girl who didn't really hang out with the other girls much," Lana explained as she told me the story. "In the past, when we had met for Bible studies or other activities, it was almost like there was a missing connection between her and everybody else. But that weekend, everything changed."

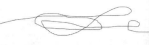

It was the final night of the camping trip, and all six young women were around a late-night fire, telling stories, giggling about the weekend's inside jokes, and asking one another questions. Eventually the talk turned to guys and relationships, and one of the girls asked Stephanie about her relationship with her boyfriend. Eric had been attending youth group and church events with Stephanie all year, but none of the other girls knew much about him.

"How's that going?" the girl had asked. Just a straightforward question.

"Bad, actually," Stephanie replied. She got right to the point. "I kind of want to break up with him, but I don't know how, and I'm honestly a little afraid to do it."

The circle of young women was quiet for a moment, then one of the other students prodded further. "What are you afraid about?"

Again, Stephanie didn't mince any words. "Honestly, Eric tries to manipulate me all the time. He's pretty controlling too. For a long time he was pressuring me to have sex, so we started doing that a while ago—I feel bad about it, but I know he won't ever want us to stop. He doesn't treat me very well, but I'm worried that if I try to end things, he won't let me. He talks about scary stuff sometimes, and it makes me think that if I dump him, he might . . . I don't know, come after me or something."

The girls leaned forward in their camp chairs. Their faces showed a sad kind of bewilderment. And they showed surprise. Stephanie had never opened up before—then again, they weren't sure any other student had asked specifically about Stephanie's life before. Or maybe she had simply reached her breaking point. For who knows how long, she had been dealing with her confusion and guilt

and fear alone, but now, possibly, she was inviting others to stand beside her. And these girls opened up to Stephanie just as readily as she had opened up to them.

"You deserve so much better than a guy who would make you afraid or who would pressure you," one of the girls said.

"It's not going to get better if you stay with him—how can we help?" another girl asked.

"I think you should call him tomorrow and break up," a third girl suggested. "We'll all sit with you and support you while you do it. Won't we, girls." That last sentence was a declaration, not a question.

Stephanie hesitated. She had a lot of options and ideas coming at her fast. "But what if he pressures me again? I'm worried I'll just keep caving in, and I won't ever be able to *really* be done with him. I'll just keep taking him back."

"You need somebody who'll support you and help you. Do you think your parents could help, maybe?"

A pause. "Yeah, probably."

"Do you think you can tell them about it?"

Another pause. "I guess I could do that, yeah."

"Well, then that's what you should do."

There were no more pauses. The second Stephanie was willing to move forward, one of the other girls was ready to charge ahead with a fully detailed plan. She was actually kind of bossy, Lana says—but it seemed like it was just what Stephanie was looking for.

"Tomorrow you're going to call him and tell him that it's over, that he's not welcome at your house ever again, and that you won't be answering his calls. And then you're going to call your mom and tell her about it. And we'll sit with you while you call and help you get through it."

The firelight shone on all six young women's faces. Five of them were fixed on Stephanie and nodding supportively. Stephanie looked amazed, appreciative, and relieved.

The next morning, back at Lana's apartment, all six young women sat in a circle and prayed together before Stephanie grabbed her cell phone and dialed Eric. She told him they were through and she would no longer tolerate any contact from him. "You don't treat me well, and I don't want to be with you." After that, she called her mom. "I just broke up with Eric. There's a lot of stuff about him that I haven't talked with you about, but he's not a nice person, and I want you to know that I don't want him to call or come around anymore. Can you help me with that?"

Stephanie stuck by her words that day, but she wasn't the only one who did. The other young women in her small group continued to support her and care about her. They asked more questions, encouraged her faith more and more, and worked harder to help her feel included. A few years later, after Stephanie fell in love with a man who cared for and cherished her, they were all at her bridal shower.

The Key Is Being Wonderfully Kind

It can be hard for us to think about confronting another person about something sinful in their life. Often that's because we think of confrontation as a "me versus them" sort of thing: putting the other person in an awkward place, judging their faults or mistakes, being critical, or potentially giving the impression that we think we're better or wiser than they are. But confrontation doesn't have to go like that. Confronting someone else could be the most loving, supportive, and generous gift you could give them.

You might see that expressed in his or her face—full of relief in the middle of an otherwise darkened night.

"We love each other because [God] loved us first," says 1 John. "And he has given us this command: Those who love God must also love their fellow believers."[54] Let's think about what that means, and let's begin by thinking about God's love.

God's love for us doesn't simply make us feel great about all the decisions we're making. It doesn't give a blanket approval for all we've ever done. No, it helps us confront our sin, and through Jesus, it gives us an exit strategy away from the effects of sin. God's love makes our hearts aware of how they're wrong, and it turns them in the right direction.

One of the things this should teach us is that if we seek to show others God's love, sometimes that love will mean confronting the effects of sin in their lives too. That can be a tricky and uncomfortable process, and since we're sinful people ourselves, we'll never be able to do it perfectly. But it *is* possible to confront sin effectively and well. The key is to let God's love be the force that steers and guides us.

Paul, in writing to the church in Rome, once had some harsh words for people who were judging others' sinfulness:

> Don't you see how wonderfully kind, tolerant, and patient God is with you? Does this mean nothing to you? Can't you see that his kindness is intended to turn you from your sin?[55]

It would be silly to suggest that what Paul is saying is that Christians shouldn't confront other Christians— Paul's ministry included regular doses of confronting other believers in their sins. Instead, part of what Paul is doing is pointing to the importance of kindness. God's kindness, he writes, is aimed at turning people away from sin.

The purpose of confrontation, when it's done with love, is to help turn people away from their sinfulness. If you love someone and you understand God's good news, then you understand that an unrepentant sinful heart separates that person from God. In other words, it will lead to their destruction. When you love someone, that's the absolute last thing you would want for them. When you love someone, you will not stand silently by as they make their death march, will you? How could that be love?

But that doesn't mean you will beat them over the head with Bible verses and calls for repentance, either. Guilt-tripping and pestering are not how God calls us to himself. No, he does it with truth demonstrated through kindness. He tells us about our sin within the gospel story of self-giving love. He proves, by reaching out to us and by wanting us, that our sin does not make us unreachable or unlovable. He patiently and gently assures us until we understand and are ready to accept him. His loving conviction stems from his kindness, which is unbelievably potent for changing hearts away from sin.

Is God leading you to confront someone in particular? Maybe their sinfulness is rearing its head through their gossiping or their exclusion of others. Maybe their sinfulness is causing them to lash out at people or do things that harm their body. Or maybe in their sinfulness they don't believe the truth that they are lovable, so like Stephanie, they're letting someone walk all over them.

If God is leading you to confront someone, begin with kindness, asking God to help you want only what's best for

the other person. Begin with an awareness of your own sinfulness, and pray that God would give you the clarity and kindness needed to speak effectively to the other person. Remember the best gift that you have ever been given—conviction over your sin and forgiveness for it—and look for opportunities to graciously tell them about that gift.

A beautiful heart confronts others'
sin and does so with kindness.

Discussion Starters

1. Proverbs 27:6 says, "Wounds from a sincere friend are better than many kisses from an enemy." How does this verse relate to the chapter we just read?

2. God's love confronts sin. What does that suggest to us if we want to share God's love with others?

3. Sadly, we often become aware of sins in others because we've sinned along with them. Are some of the sins you've seen in others' lives sins that you need to repent of too?

22

A *Heart* That Forgives

Over a Jacket:
A Terrible-to-Beautiful
Story

"This is important!" my friend Rachel kept saying. Her voice was a little raised—urgent—and she was holding on to my wrist adamantly. "You need this!"

She was right, but she also wasn't, and that made for a pretty terrible interaction between the two of us that day. Later, though, it led to a beautiful one.

For a while after my accident, it was difficult for me to show my left arm out in public. Sometimes I still find it a little challenging, but far less often and far less strongly now than I used to. In the beginning, the idea of showing my arm to other people seemed almost impossible.

It's hard to explain why it was such a struggle, except to say that it was a *process*. I needed to adjust to my new reality, and that was taking time. I had spent over twenty years getting used to one way of life. It included an arm

years getting used to one way of life. It included an arm

173

that looked and functioned like *that*, and now all of a sudden my arm looked and functioned like *this*. But along with that, my arm was just one of *many* trauma-related issues that needed to be addressed.

There were three in particular. One, I was learning to trust God in my painful new circumstances. Two, my physical healing was underway (but not yet complete). Three, I faced intense emotional effects following my accident. Not only did those three impact my recovery most, together they also led to plenty of stress for one person. So I was dealing with them first, and I was willing to put off other concerns to do so. Even the question of how I would manage my left arm in public had to be secondary.

One day, probably sooner rather than later, I would need to accept the new look and the new functionality of my left arm. I'd need to learn how to interact socially without wearing a prosthesis too. I knew I would do those things eventually. I was even taking baby steps toward them when I felt like I could. But although they had their place on my to-do list, it was still too much to try to focus on my three priorities *and* focus on my arm.

That was where I was when Rachel and I went shopping together one Saturday in Dallas. We had decided it was a good day for another baby step, so I had intentionally left my prosthesis behind. I wore a light, long-sleeved jacket instead—my arm was covered by a sleeve, but going out like that was still a big step for me.

Since Rachel and I had planned the jacket-instead-of-prosthesis thing ahead of time, I assumed we were on the same page about it. We weren't.

At one point in the afternoon, we stopped, and Rachel told me I should take the jacket off and keep going in the

short-sleeved shirt I had on underneath. "You don't even have to think about it, just do it," she kept insisting. "It's what you need right now!"

But it wasn't. That day I had only thought about wearing the jacket. Trying to deal with short sleeves in public was still *way* more than I needed.

I argued with her, saying I wasn't ready. She didn't agree. I turned away, attempting to walk on, and she jumped in front of me so I couldn't get by. It was awkward. But I did *not* want to do what she was telling me to do, so I kept resisting. And she kept trying to change my mind. We argued and bickered, and neither of us would budge. It went on like that for a little while, with other nearby shoppers obviously eavesdropping on the whole interaction. By the time our shopping expedition ended, Rachel and I were both frustrated, and I was in tears.

When Rachel and I saw each other again a couple of days later, I was shocked to find out that she already assumed that our friendship was over. She felt badly for pushing too hard, and she figured that I would certainly cut her off for good. In her mind, that was it: friendship finished. No chance of reconciling. No hope to move forward.

Over an arm and a jacket.

The thing is, Rachel hasn't had a lot of experience with people who know God. When we met, she hadn't had much personal experience with God, period. What she had seen in her relationships and in her history was that the world works like this: If you hurt someone, it creates a rift forever.

When she explained this to me, though, it sounded silly in light of the gospel. "You have to be willing to accept grace from me," I told her. "It can be hard doing that sometimes, but it's just part of living life together and giving friendship a chance."

The concept was straightforward and almost obvious to me. I might have even said it with a few shrugs. But it hit Rachel like a ton of bricks. She didn't know how to respond; at first she could only be quiet. When I asked her what she was thinking, all she could say was, "I don't really know."

She figured it out later and sent me an e-mail expressing her thoughts. After admitting that she had considered ending our friendship over the disagreement, she expressed that it had rocked her to realize I didn't feel the same way. In a situation like the one we had just been through, she fully expected that I would write her out of my life completely. When I didn't, she was floored. The way she put it was, "I've never experienced that type of grace before."

I've never experienced that type of grace. How awful! How saddening! Rachel couldn't even fathom being forgiven by someone. Not even by someone who cared about her. Not even over a jacket.

Just imagine how awful it would be if the world actually did work like that.

How Do Your Sins Rank?

Jesus shows us in John 8 that responding to another person's sinfulness requires a ranking system. And, no, that doesn't mean we should be weighing other people's sin against our own in order to decide who's better and who's worse. That isn't even possible with the ranking system Jesus offers because that system has only two categories: Yes and No.

In this story, some of the religious leaders in Jesus'

time seek out Jesus at the Temple and basically hurl a woman in front of him. She has been caught cheating on her husband—*Adultery!*—they announce. They add that Jewish law states that for this the woman should be stoned to death immediately. *What does Jesus have to say about it?* they wonder.

Jesus' response is fascinating. The Bible says that all he does is kneel down and, with his finger, begin writing in the dust. We don't know any details about what he was writing—for all we know, it could've been a recipe for roast lamb. But we do know that he writes, and soon after that, something changes in the crowd.

When the religious leaders have had enough of Jesus' dusty silence, they demand that he give them an answer. *Should we stone her, or what?* Jesus speaks up after that, and it's not at all what they expect: "All right, but let the one who has never sinned throw the first stone!"[56] Then he writes in the dust a little longer.

Here's what the passage says happens next:

> When the accusers heard this, they slipped away one by one, beginning with the oldest, until only Jesus was left in the middle of the crowd with the woman. Then Jesus stood up again and said to the woman, "Where are your accusers? Didn't even one of them condemn you?"
>
> "No, Lord," she said.
>
> And Jesus said, "Neither do I. Go and sin no more."[57]

Let's summarize for a moment. People catch someone else in sin. They know the sin deserves to be punished. They come to Jesus, demanding punishment, and he (1) writes in the dust and (2) tells them that the sinless ones among them can throw stones all they want.

Throw stones all you want—there! That's the crux of this story. What Jesus is saying here is that if you're sinless you have the right to throw stones. Of course, after that, every one of this woman's accusers walks away from her. But that's not the most significant part of the story, because after her accusers fly the coop, the sinful woman is left beside the one man who is actually a God-man. Who is actually sinless.

Standing there, Jesus is completely justified in punishing sin. Sin, after all, is what will eventually kill him. But Jesus refuses to give the woman instant death for her sins. Instead, he will take her death sentence for himself. He will choose to be humiliated and betrayed and rejected even more than she has been, in order to offer her life. In order to offer every accuser life too.

The basic message that Jesus gives to the woman's accusers that day is something we should all seek to apply in our own lives: We have no right to judge others. We, too, are marred by sin and could be caught red-handed in it just as easily as she was. But that's a minor point to focus on in the story. Jesus' other message from that day is even more striking: "Neither do I [condemn you]. Go and sin no more."

In hearing Jesus' words to this sinful woman, we must remember that he says the same words to us. Like her, we stand accused by our sinfulness, and our sin carries a price that must somehow be paid. Like her, we deserve death. But we have been set free, and the high cost of our sin has been covered by someone else! Because of that, our changed hearts should want to do more than just turn away from blame and judgment when it comes to others' sins. Jesus' response to the woman caught in adultery—and to *us*—makes us people who can forgive. How could we, as

sinners, condemn another sinner when we have been un-deservedly forgiven by the perfect, sinless One?

> *A beautiful heart not only doesn't*
> *judge others' sin; it forgives.*

Discussion Starters

1. What are the two messages that Jesus presents in the story of the woman caught in adultery? (Hint: One is to the religious leaders; one is to the woman.) Why is it necessary for us to see that *both* these messages apply to us?

2. Who is someone in your life that you need to forgive? Do you think of yourself as a sinner, just like they are, or do you tend to think of yourself as better than they are?

3. Hurts happen in every relationship. How can you foster a spirit of forgiveness with the people you care about most? With the people who've hurt you most?

Part Five

Your Distinctive Heart

WE ARE GOD'S
MASTERPIECE.

EPHESIANS 2:10

23

A *Heart* That Delights

What Will They Think?: A Familiar Story

Mermaids aren't real, but apparently mermaid tails are. One of my good friends knows a teenage girl, Brynne, who lives on the East Coast and is involved in a couple of uncommon interests and activities. To be more precise, Brynne is more than just *involved*. She has thrown herself into some unique pursuits all by herself, without caring what anybody else might think about them. One of those pursuits involves a mermaid tail.

A while ago, Brynne found out about a company that tailor-makes mermaid tails for people. Not only are the tails one of a kind and perfectly fitted for one person's body, but with a little training and practice, you can actually swim in them. Brynne loved everything about this idea. She got herself hooked on it.

The thing is, custom mermaid tails can be expensive.

Most people probably wouldn't even consider spending that much money on something so out of the norm. And many teen girls might be discouraged from buying one, not only because of the cost but also because it's different from what other people are doing. After all, there's no telling how your peers will respond—will they think it's cool, or will they mock you?—when you've slipped into a swim tail that covers half your body.

But Brynne wanted a mermaid tail because *she* loved the idea. She didn't care how any other person would respond to it. She thought it would be a blast to have one and to dive into a pool with it. So she saved and saved her money, and eventually she bought herself a tail.

It's a piece of her own real-life fairy tale when Brynne slips into a pool and dolphin-kicks her way across the water. Even walking to the water's edge (yes, it is possible for her to walk in the tail) is more fun than she expected. And when observers see the way she enjoys her time in it, they can't help but come away impressed. It makes people happy to see a girl who is happy and isn't afraid to have her originality stand out. She isn't bothered about the things that might make her different, and instead she goes ahead and lets them shine.

There have been plenty of days lately that I wish I knew how to be more like Brynne. While I don't have trouble standing out in certain ways, like with my fashion choices or certain less-than-popular activities (longboard skateboarding and boxing are just two of the ways I like to spend my time), it can still be exceptionally hard for me to stand out in other ways. The most common example is that it's a struggle for me to think that I might stand out because of my left arm.

One day during my recovery, I was talking with Brittany and Shaun, expressing some details of my struggle. I was afraid, worried that because my arm looks different from most people's, the different factor might cause guys to react to me in a negative way. My worry about this had become a long list of questions:

If a guy sees me without my prosthesis, what's he going to think?
Does it freak a guy out to see a girl who has only one hand?
How does that change the way a guy will see me?
Will he treat me differently?
Will I be rejected or coddled because of this?
Will I ever be able to feel "normal" in a relationship and not worry about how my arm looks?

All these questions felt like they were spinning on a never-ending loop in my mind. They felt like a weight pressing on my chest, consuming me. They had me *so* worried. Something about me was different, and it made me fear that people would think I was "less" of a person in some way. It made me afraid that this difference would somehow limit things and get in the way of my relationships.

What I didn't realize that day was that there was a deeper fear happening in me. This fear had nothing to do with my left arm. Instead, it was a fear that happens in all of us, no matter who we are or what we face. Often we can't see it because it hides under the surface, but we see the evidence of it in many of the other insecurity weeds that grow in our lives.

This deeper fear is the soil that our other insecurities are rooted in. It is the thing that feeds them and causes them to thrive and bloom. And *it*—not the traits or interests or experiences that might make us different—is the thing we ultimately have to deal with.

Getting to the root of this issue is the only thing that will make the difference.

Dead on Arrival

Here is the root: We get insecure about what other people think of us because, deep down, we are insecure about what *God* thinks of us. We become afraid that we won't measure up with people because we're afraid that we can't measure up with God. We're supersensitive about the things that make us different among other people because we're scared to death of being deficient in front of God. Of being not enough for him. Of being unwanted and unworthy.

There is something in us that is always, always trying to prove ourselves to God, and at the same time there is something in us that knows we have absolutely no idea how to do that. On our own and at our core, we know we can't be pleasing enough to make our Creator accept us. Nobody has to teach us that; it's ingrained in us because sin makes it the basic truth about us. No wonder we tend to run around like little flurries of insecurity!

But there is a basic truth about God that is bigger than this basic truth about us. This is the truth that kills insecurity at its root. Here's how Ephesians 2 explains it:

> *Once you were dead because of your disobedience and your many sins. You used to live in sin, just like the rest of the world. . . . All of us used to live that way, following the passionate desires and inclinations of our sinful*

nature. By our very nature we were subject to God's anger, just like everyone else.[58]

What this passage points out is that simply being who we are makes us subject to God's anger. Basically what that means is this: Because of our sinfulness, we deserve to die. There's that basic truth about us. Then—*phew!*—there's a "but."

> *But God is so rich in mercy, and he loved us so much, that even though we were dead because of our sins, he gave us life when he raised Christ from the dead. . . . For he raised us from the dead along with Christ and seated us with him in the heavenly realms because we are united with Christ Jesus. So God can point to us in all future ages as examples of the incredible wealth of his grace and kindness toward us, as shown in all he has done for us who are united with Christ Jesus.*[59]

Our sinfulness makes us as good as dead, but God's love for us gives us life. By uniting us with Jesus, God gives us the identity he wants for us. He chooses to see us not based on who we are, but on who Christ is. He doesn't look at our deficiencies. Instead, he shows us off as evidence of amazing things: God's grace, God's kindness, and the good work that Jesus has done. Later in the passage, it's described like this: "We are God's masterpiece."[60]

If we have received Jesus' gift of salvation, this means that when God looks at us, he doesn't see our deficiencies. He doesn't see people who don't measure up. He doesn't see people who can never be good enough. What he sees is that we are seated next to Jesus! He delights in looking at us.

The ultimate and basic question we have about ourselves, about measuring up to God, has been answered. We are sitting before him, united with the One who has the seat of total honor. We have all the acceptance and approval that anyone could need. Part of what this means is that there shouldn't be any food at the roots of our other insecurities, helping them grow. It shouldn't matter whether other people might come up with reasons to disapprove of us.

God delights in us. That defines us as people who should be delighted in. Other people might or might not grasp that concept. But *we* can and should. Because God delights in us, we can learn to delight in ourselves.

We can appreciate ourselves, regardless of what any other person says or what any dark corner of our own hearts wants to believe. We can enjoy what's different about us, without fearing disapproval or rejection, because we have the best approval and the final acceptance. We don't have to worry about what anyone else will think about us. Our Creator has already given his verdict with a flourish: In love and with his own Son's blood, he has signed his name on us, his finest work of art.

A beautiful heart doesn't need approval or acceptance from others, for it knows it is God's masterpiece.

Discussion Starters

1. What are some of the insecurities you face? According to this chapter, what is at the root of them? How do you see that this is true?

2. How does Ephesians 2 show us that we don't need to be afraid of being unworthy of God? Do you believe that? Why or why not?

3. How would things change for you if you thought of yourself as God's masterpiece? How would knowing you have God's approval change some of your insecurities?

Beauty *plus* FULL:
you have to have both parts
to get to
BEAUTIFUL

24

A *Heart* That Fills Up

Two Kinds of Compliments:
A "Beautiful" Story

"I love your shoes!"
   "Such a sweet smile."
   "Beautiful blonde hair."
   "Great style!"

When I was a teenager, I received compliments on my looks fairly often. I don't like bringing this up, but it's impossible for me to tell this story without doing so. (Bear with me!) It wasn't uncommon for friends and even strangers to come up to me and tell me they liked something about my physical appearance. Which sounds like the kind of problem any girl would love to have, right? Well, maybe not.

The compliments I received became a problem in my heart. A big problem. Not because the compliments themselves were bad or harmful, but because the compliments *plus* my sinful heart were a poisonous combo.

191

Even though I've always liked fashion and experimenting with clothing combinations, I've never been the kind of girl who likes primping or spending a lot of time in front of a mirror. Soaking up compliments about my looks didn't turn me into that kind of person, but it *did* change me. It began gripping its fingers around my heart, instilling in me a value of my appearance that was way out of balance.

I began putting pressure on myself to always be dressed and styled a certain way. I was more and more aware of people's reactions to my appearance, and those reactions mattered to me more and more. I began to let my looks define me, until they had become a pretty powerful idol in my life.

Then, with the flash of a propeller, everything changed.

There were times after my accident when, waking up from sleep, I felt that I must have dreamed what had happened to me. Like it hadn't all been real. In many respects, I'm sure I wanted it not to be real. But no, I'd wake up and it was always another real morning or afternoon or evening, and my hand and eye were both really missing, and half my hair really was shaved off. My idol didn't have any satisfying answers for me about all that.

If I had tried to survive my recovery based on my idol's rules, with my worth stemming from how I looked, then there wouldn't have been much hope for me lying there like that. Based on what our culture expects beauty to look like, what I saw in my mirror those days was pretty rough. I had dark scars; I didn't have flouncy, evenly cut hair or a symmetrical face; and my left arm stopped just above my wrist.

Still, the way I looked then was exactly what caused

my idol to start toppling, because looking like I did was a big part of what caused God's work to happen so solidly in my heart. Based on appearance alone, I didn't feel beautiful, but I began to see that the work God was doing in me was exquisite. It was far more beautiful than any kind of looks-based beauty I had ever seen or experienced. There was no question; I knew I wanted to be *this* kind of beautiful.

That's not to say that my idol was crushed instantly. It takes time and pain for an idol to go away.

Several months after God began breaking things down in my heart, I was sitting with my dad outside in my parents' backyard. It was sunny and warm, like Dallas usually is, so the shirt I was wearing was sleeveless. I looked down at my left arm at one point and felt overcome by insecurity about it. I let my thoughts pour out into the air between my dad and me, bluntly and plainly. I was talking in idol terms: questioning how people would react to my arm, worrying what others might think, wondering how I would handle any negative reactions.

My dad stopped me. His response was matter-of-fact and definite. "Lauren, your arm is so beautiful."

Just like that. Like it was the simplest, most obvious thing ever. In the best way possible, those six words sliced right through me.

My dad's compliment was rooted in what is true: that God's work is beautiful, and that God's presence in a person is what makes them beautiful. My dad wasn't looking at my arm and seeing merely a body part that's shaped one way or another; he was looking at my arm and seeing the story God had been writing all around it. He was seeing my increased reliance on Jesus, my added closeness to God, and my still-growing faith. He was seeing what mattered about my arm, and everything that mattered was found beneath the surface.

But there was more to my dad's comment than that. Part of what he was saying was that my left arm is actually, visually beautiful. He meant it exactly like that. What that tells me is that he hadn't bought into our culture's shallow and narrow-minded concept of beauty. Not one bit. His definition of *beautiful* was something deeper.

Words can't express how much that single compliment from my dad has been changing me. Months have passed since we talked that day in the backyard, and God is still using what my dad said to help me see myself and my appearance differently. God has been using it to turn my idol-loving heart more and more toward the truth, and I couldn't ask for anything better. Thankfully, shallow compliments aren't the only ones that soak in.

Miracles of Bread and Beauty

We need to take a close look at this word *beautiful*. "Beauty-full" is what it means. Filled to the brim—so much beauty that there's no room to add any more.

Our world and our hearts are confused about this word. Look around: We have billion-dollar hair, makeup, and clothing industries; racks and racks of magazines featuring airbrushed models in every store; cosmetic surgery growing in popularity each day; and people being praised, rewarded, and idolized simply because their physical features are shaped in certain ways. It's all ridiculous.

Before we put the blame on just our culture, though, it's important to also look at our own hearts. We obsess about pimples, freckles, frizz, nose shape, eye color, neck

length, hip width, chest measurements, waistlines, weight loss, weight gain, hair color, hair texture, shoe size—anything, everything. We compare ourselves to models, actresses, athletes, friends, and strangers across the room, always finding ways that we don't measure up to their beauty.

Will we ever feel satisfied with how we look? Will our appearance ever seem good enough? Will this constant need to improve the externals ever go away?

To answer those questions, let's go back to *beautiful*. A gigantic problem in our world and in ourselves is that we don't see that beauty and fullness go together. Beauty *plus* full: You have to have both parts to get to beautiful.

Our culture and our hearts seem convinced that beauty *equals* fullness. We behave as if the two words mean the same thing. Even worse, we behave as if the shallowest and most fleeting kind of beauty, a person's appearance, guarantees fullness. Our obsession with the mirror and our near-constant, pit-of-the-stomach, I'm-never-pretty-enough feelings prove this.

But feeling even deeply, despairingly displeased about our appearance doesn't actually say anything about our looks. It doesn't prove we're not pretty. What it says instead is that inside each one of us, we ache for something. We believe that a pleasing physical appearance can take that ache away.

In other words, we have a cosmic emptiness, and we've bought into the idea that being "good-looking" is what will fill us. It won't. It can't.

John 6 tells the story of how Jesus took a little boy's meal, five loaves of bread and two fish, and miraculously divided it up so it fed five thousand people.[61] The next day,

the passage tells us, people from that same group followed Jesus to a new place and asked him for another
miracle. They hint at what they want that miracle to be,
reminding Jesus that when Moses led God's people, there
was miracle-bread to eat every day.[62] Here's how the story
continues:

> *Jesus said, "I tell you the truth, Moses didn't give you*
> *bread from heaven. My Father did. And now he offers*
> *you the true bread from heaven. The true bread of God*
> *is the one who comes down from heaven and gives life*
> *to the world."*
>
> *"Sir," they said, "give us that bread every day."*
>
> *Jesus replied, "I am the bread of life. Whoever comes*
> *to me will never be hungry again. Whoever believes in*
> *me will never be thirsty."*[63]

We've seen a conversation similar to this before, when
Jesus spoke with the Samaritan woman at the well. Once
again, here we see people asking Jesus for one thing—in
this case, bread—and they're told in reply that what they
need is not bread but Jesus. Essentially, his message here
is this: Bread will make you feel full for a little while, but I
will fill you up so your hunger is gone forever.

Imagine moving this conversation to our day and age.
A group of young women approach Jesus and one of them
says, "Lord, would you please make us look beautiful?"
Everything around them is telling them that outer beauty
is what they need. They believe that getting more and more
of it will take away the ache they feel deep within.

But Jesus knows that feeling pretty is not the same
as being full, even though it might make someone feel
full for a little while. Jesus knows that the deepest ache a

young woman feels is her ache for him. "Come to me," he might tell her, "and you will stop longing to look different than you do." He says, "I am the beauty you want and the fullness you seek."

A beautiful heart finds fullness in Jesus, not in a certain kind of physical appearance.

Discussion Starters

1. When you think of the word *beautiful*, what do you typically think of? In what ways have you seen yourself or others living as if beauty equals fullness?

2. When the people ask Jesus for bread, how does he respond? What does his response teach them about himself? What does it teach them about themselves?

3. How did God use Lauren's conversation with her dad to help show her what "beautiful" really means? How might having a correct understanding of "beautiful" change how you look at yourself?

WHATEVER GOD HAS
PLACED IN YOU—ANY
SKILL, EXPERIENCE,
OR DREAM—CAN BE
USED FOR HIS

Glory

AND THE
WORLD'S GOOD.

25

A *Heart* That Dreams

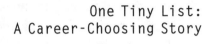

**One Tiny List:
A Career-Choosing Story**

"What do you want to be when you grow up?"

Like all teenagers and young adults, I was asked this question countless times during middle school, high school, college, and even after that. But even though I had a good idea of what I wanted to do with my life, professionally speaking, for a long time I had difficulty answering the question. I thought that as a Christian, there were only a few appropriate responses to it, and I knew mine wasn't one of those few.

It often seemed like the only careers I heard talked about in church or at my Christian school were "full-time Christian ministry" careers. In other words, doctors and nurses who worked with the poor in third-world countries, pastors, missionaries to far-flung places, worship leaders, Bible study teachers, church planters, Christian school

workers, musicians in Christian bands, and people who helped run nonprofit Christian organizations. That was pretty much it. The fact that the list was always so short, with always the same careers on it, left me with the impression that a Christian young woman had only a small cluster of God-approved pursuits to choose from.

Disheartening, to say the least.

It's not that I didn't like or approve of those career paths—in fact, I thought all of them seemed pretty amazing, for lots of different reasons. The problem was that I couldn't see how any of those options had anything to do with the dreams in my heart or the talents God had given me. I felt like I had two bad options: I could set aside my own unique interests and skills in order to follow one of the career paths that had earned the short list's okay, or by going in a direction that seemed much better suited for me, I could put myself in an "un-Christian" field that had "un-Christian" pursuits.

In my view, those really were the only two options. Trying to somehow have the best of both worlds—a real, God-focused ministry *and* a career that would make me want to jump excitedly out of bed every morning—seemed impossible. After all, when's the last time you heard of a job opening for a missionary fashion merchandiser? How about a church accessories specialist?

Then a little book called *Roaring Lambs* made its way into my life. It was written by a man named Bob Briner, who was not only an Emmy-winning TV producer but also a strong Christian. Mr. Briner made the case in his book that Christians are needed everywhere and that Christians have a mission field in every industry, not just in places where most people are carrying a Bible already. He highlighted

many passages in Scripture, showing that God's people should rush into their world[64]—into jobs and careers where they're side by side with people who need Jesus. We should be where God has gifted and called us to be, and there we should do all that we can do to roar our Shepherd's good news.

Although Briner's message liberated me, I quickly discovered that not all the Christians I knew were on board with it. When I was preparing to live and intern in New York for the first time, there were a number of people who expressed concerns for me, both in conversations with me and with my parents. They worried that the fashion and entertainment industries might tarnish my faith or lure me away from Jesus. They feared that I would be the only Christian in my workplace and that such an environment would make it too easy to back down on my standards or even to abandon my love for God.

I knew, though, that as much as God had inclined my heart toward these industries in New York, he had drawn my heart toward himself even more. I wasn't worried about the impact that the city might have on me, because I was focused on what God might do in and through me. My eyes weren't primarily on the career opportunities or the geography; they were primarily on him. As far as I was concerned, the location and the job specifics were just background information for the *real* story God would be writing on my life and on the lives of those I would meet.

What I found while working in New York was that there weren't a lot of Christians in the industry, but there were some. They were in all different kinds of roles: assistants, designers, models, TV crew members, actors, buyers, administrators. And you know what? They weren't outcasts, and they weren't thought of as boring or prudes. People respected them, listened to them, and went to them for help or advice. You could tell these believers looked for opportunities to care for others with God's care and to share with others God's love.

Many of the Christians I met in the entertainment industry shone brightly in largely dark places. Every time I saw it, I was grateful for it. I was glad God was giving me the chance—*within* my career dreams, no less—to add some flickers too.

At the Center of His Work

I don't know how we church people let ourselves believe that only certain jobs and professions (for that matter, hobbies and interests and pastimes too) are useful in God's hands. If we read the Bible, we have no reason to come away from it with that impression.

Take multicolored-coat Joseph, for example. Even after Joseph was sold by his brothers into slavery, accused of a serious crime, thrown into prison, and all but forgotten there, Genesis shows us that God used Joseph to have serious impact for him and for his Kingdom. His influence began in Egypt, while he was working as a servant in the house of Potiphar, the captain of Pharaoh's guard:

> The LORD was with Joseph, so he succeeded in
> everything he did as he served in the home of his
> Egyptian master. Potiphar noticed this and realized
> that the LORD was with Joseph, giving him success
> in everything he did. This pleased Potiphar, so he soon
> made Joseph his personal attendant. . . . So Potiphar
> gave Joseph complete administrative responsibility over

everything he owned. With Joseph there, he didn't worry
about a thing—except what kind of food to eat![65]

Unfortunately, next comes that serious (and false) accusation about Joseph, and he is undeservedly thrown into prison. But even there, he has much influence. God causes the prison warden to appreciate Joseph, and eventually he's put in charge of all the other prisoners.

Already, Joseph and his faith in God have played a pivotal role in the lives of a high-ranking military official and his whole household, a civil leader (the warden), and who knows how many prisoners. But God's work through Joseph isn't nearly finished yet.

Having made some connections in prison and having interpreted some dreams for fellow prisoners there, Joseph eventually lands in Pharaoh's palace to interpret two of the king's own dreams. Joseph is the only person who is able to interpret them, correctly predicting to Pharaoh that Egypt will experience seven years of prosperity, with seven years of famine to follow. After interpreting the dream, Joseph goes on to advise Pharaoh on what should be done during those fourteen years in order for his country to not only survive famine but thrive. Pharaoh's response to all this is fantastic:

> *Pharaoh asked his officials, "Can we find anyone else*
> *like this man so obviously filled with the spirit of God?"*
> *Then Pharaoh said to Joseph, "Since God has revealed*
> *the meaning of the dreams to you, clearly no one else is*
> *as intelligent or wise as you are. You will be in charge of*
> *my court, and all my people will take orders from you.*
> *Only I, sitting on my throne, will have a rank higher*
> *than yours."*[66]

But even *that* isn't the end of what God has in store. With Joseph serving essentially as the prime minister of Egypt and sitting at the helm of its famine-survival program, the country eventually becomes the destination that people from all around must travel to for food. Among those who trek to Egypt and buy food from its storehouses are some brothers, the sons of a man named Israel. These are the same brothers who betrayed Joseph and sold him years earlier, but more important, they are the family who carry God's covenant promise. Through this family's descendants, all nations of the earth will be blessed.[67]

After some interesting events (fake accusations of spying, the brothers being thrown into prison, a trip to Canaan and back, and both money and a silver cup being hidden in sacks of grain—read the story!), Joseph and his brothers are restored to one another. The brothers return to their father with food and with the promise that they will make it through the famine. How? The whole family is about to be moved to a land near the Nile that will be good for their flocks, courtesy of an Egyptian wagon caravan ordered by Pharaoh himself.

So the covenant will live on through this family, just as God has said it will. And now it will rightfully include Joseph and his two sons,[68] who have been brought back into the fold and who now can take part in blessing all nations, just as God promised that Israel and his descendants would. This means that by the end of Joseph's life, the reach of his influence has gone from nothing (abandoned in a pit), to a prominent household, to the king's prison, to a palace, to a kingdom, to all nations. All of it had been carved out by God as part of his plan.

God could have revealed his Spirit to Pharaoh using no one. He could have provided food to surrounding nations using no one. He could have rescued Israel's family and protected his covenant with them (and his promised blessing to all!) using no one. He chose to use a person. Not only that, but in this instance, he didn't use a prophet or a priest or a traveling missionary or a pastor or a Bible teacher—although we know from elsewhere in the Bible that each of those roles is important. No. In Joseph, God has at the center of his work a military assistant, a diplomat, a politician.

So we see, directly from Scripture, that we don't have to be in a specifically religious role for it to be ministry. Whatever God has placed in you—any skill, any experience, any dream, and even a responsibility that might surprise you—he can use for his glory and the world's good. The question is not what your job or title or activity is, but how God is using it to work through you.

A beautiful heart understands that God's purposes can be accomplished within many roles and a wide variety of work.

Discussion Starters

1. What are some of the dreams God seems to have placed in your heart? Have you ever doubted that God could work through them?

2. What positions did Joseph hold throughout his story, and how did God use them?

3. Looking at Joseph's life, how do you think we should understand the word *ministry*? What does that mean for potential ministry opportunities in your life?

26

A Heart That Dares

Defying the Obstacles: A Surfing Story

Sharks lurking underwater. More and more of them, always unseen, potentially everywhere. And that was just the start of it.

My friend Bethany Hamilton had her left arm taken off in a tiger shark attack in the Hawaiian surf when she was thirteen years old. That was on the last day of October, 2003. Less than a month later, on November 26, she was back in the water and back on her board. She wanted to become a pro surfer one day—that had been her goal before the bite, and it was still her goal afterward.

There had been one other big goal in her life too, before the bite, and that one didn't change either.

In the last two weeks of October, the two weeks leading up to the shark attack, Bethany and her mom had been praying every day that God would reveal to Bethany his plan

for her life. She loved Jesus and was committed to serving him, and she wanted God to show her how she could best do that. She knew she had a passion for surfing and a natural skill on the waves, and she knew she wanted to help introduce other people to Jesus—but she didn't have a clear picture of how God wanted those things to go together.

After that giant fish snapped its jaws around her left arm, the picture started becoming clearer.

Many of us already know how Bethany's story continued after her attack. She went back to surfing almost immediately. She won the national title for surfing in the United States just two years after losing her arm. Her dream of going pro came true. And she became well-known around the globe, traveling the world, making TV appearances, and earning countless awards. Everywhere she's been, from orphanages and disaster areas to surf competitions to NBC and MTV, she has brought God's message of love. For the last decade, Bethany has been a surfing ambassador for Jesus.

But nobody knew that was how things would turn out in the beginning, when her bandages were still on and she hadn't had the chance to go back to her boards. In the beginning, it was the obstacles that seemed most obvious.

For starters, there were the practical, water-and-board obstacles. *How do you work up the courage to go back into the ocean, knowing what could lurk underneath? And even if you do dare get back in, how do you manage to get back up on your board? How do you keep your balance, with one arm completely gone? How do you duck-dive (under crashing waves) with your board, with only one hand to hold it? How do you get to the top of the pack in your sport while possibly relearning everything?*

But potentially bigger than the surfing obstacles were the God obstacles. Plenty of people who heard Bethany's story were mystified about those. *How do you put your trust in a God who lets something so horrible occur? How do you commit your life to God, knowing that such awful things might still happen? How do you dare continue on, thinking you can be obedient and happy with him?*

The thing was, though, God had put a love of surfing in Bethany that was bigger than any fear about sharks, standing up on a board again, or getting herself under a wave. And God had assured Bethany that his love for her was far too great and strong to be sidelined by the loss of an arm. Or by even the loss of her whole surfing life, if it would come to that.

Bethany had nightmares for a while after her attack, reliving some of her trauma. She had to demote herself to beginner surfboards as she learned how to balance again. She got tossed by some big waves, trying to duck-dive one-handed while paddling out. But none of it stopped her. She kept her face pointed toward the unique passion that God had given her. It seemed he was still leading her toward surfing, so she dared to keep at it, defying the obstacles in her way.

The other thing she kept doing didn't come quite so naturally to her. If Bethany could've picked a way to be used by God, it probably wouldn't have had anything to do with making TV appearances, filming movies, or being famous. She doesn't love the spotlight of fame and would likely live a much more quiet life if it were up to her. That said, she's not about to let her own personality preferences keep her from doing the ministry that God has plopped so clearly into her lap.

She throws herself into the opportunities she's given—gladly and with a heart of joy. You see, when Bethany prayed at thirteen for God to reveal his plan for her life, she meant it. She wanted *his* plan, even if that meant it would be different from hers. That's why she charges out into the waves with only one arm, and it's why she charges ahead into Hollywood and elsewhere, despite how camera-shy she might feel.

Bethany dares to follow God wherever he leads her, no matter what he asks of her and no matter how hard it gets. She trusts the Bible when it says that God will take *everything* and work it out for good in the lives of people who love him and are called to his purpose.[69] In her own words, "If I didn't have one arm, I wouldn't be sharing God's Word with everyone. And God put me on this earth to serve him, and he's gone through so much worse things than what I've gone through. . . . Having one arm is the way he uses me."[70]

Our Incredible Shrinking Obstacles

What's your obstacle to following God faithfully? It might be your fear of rejection by family or friends or our culture. It might be your thoughts that you're somehow inadequate for the task. It might be a feeling that you must have all the answers figured out and clarified before you'll be ready to jump in. It might be your worry that following God will limit other hopes and dreams in your heart. It might be that you're afraid God will let you down. Or it might be that you're used to *not* following, so you're not sure how to get started.

Whatever our obstacle(s) may be, and whether they're mentioned above or not, there's one simple thing that will give us the strength and motivation to follow God when obstacles threaten to get in our way. Bethany knows what it is, because she makes a point to mention it. Do you see? What she says is, "He's gone through so much worse."

God the Father and Jesus the Son both went through the worst that the universe has to offer, all because of their love for us. Jesus went to the cross and died the worst kind of death imaginable, feeling every moment of torturous pain in his body. Before that, he let himself be brutalized by Roman guards, including lashings designed to tear through his flesh. But the beatings and the crucifixion were just the start of it. With his last breath on the cross, Jesus surrendered his perfect life to the full penalty of sin. The Bible tells us that darkness covered the whole land for three hours leading up to that ultimate event.

The moment was obscenely unfair and despicably, tormentingly wrong. But Jesus bore it, willingly, for us. Not only that, but as he did, his Father refused to rescue him. Imagine how it must have broken God's heart to keep from protecting his beloved Son! To deny Jesus the love and rescue that he had earned fully. But he did. They both did. Because they love us. Nothing stopped them from their intent to offer us the salvation we need. No obstacle could get in the way.

When we have God's sacrifice in mind, the obstacles we face in following God's plan begin to seem smaller and smaller, even minuscule. No matter how insurmountable anything in our lives might seem, we see that it's nothing in light of what God himself has endured. He refused to give up on the ones he loves, all the way to the point of his death. We can learn from him and express our gratitude for this by following him faithfully for life.

Pursuing God this way requires us to be daring in two ways. The first kind of boldness is a mental step: trusting

God's leading in our lives and believing we're safe on the path he has put us on. Jesus' sacrifice has shown us that God wants the best for us and will do anything and everything to make sure we can get it. We have no reason to believe that he will leave us hurt or stranded. He equips our feet perfectly for whatever roads he asks us to walk. When we feel unsure, we must dare to believe that he is our sureness.

The second kind of daring is the action itself: daring to face our obstacles head-on, not letting them scare us away. This second kind of daring is what proves that the first kind is real. It is trust come alive. And it's the natural result of seeing how God's plans for us are daring beyond our wildest dreams. With our eyes on him, we can be daring too.

A beautiful heart dares to trust God's leading, plowing through obstacles that seem to stand in the way.

Discussion Starters

1. What are some of the obstacles that hinder or keep you from following God faithfully? How do they typically get in the way?

2. What does it mean that God didn't let any obstacles get in the way of his love for us? How do we see that?

3. Knowing how God dares for us, how should that change how we dare for him? What's one area of your life where you want to dare for God? How can you start?

27

A *Heart* That Includes

Scratching the Surface:
An Exclusion Story

"How'd it go?"
"What did you do?"
"Who did you meet?"
"When did you get back?"
"Which experiences were your favorites?"
All questions that nobody asked.

When I was in college and working to make a start in the fashion industry, every season I would travel to New York for Fashion Week. While in the city, it was my job to visit different shows and events in order to report on them later. When I wasn't on assignment, I took advantage of the fact that nearly the entire US fashion industry had converged on the city at once. I arranged meetings, sparked networking opportunities, and browsed displays whenever possible, eager to soak up all I could.

Fashion Week was an electrifying time for someone like me. It seemed to offer endless opportunities for learning more and connecting with people who were thriving in the field that I loved. As far as the clothing was concerned, it could always be counted on to showcase upcoming trends and daring risks, not to mention classic staples, retro styles, and an abundance of surprises. All of it was a feast for the design-loving eye.

There was only one thing wrong with my Fashion Week adventures: the post-adventure part. Each time I'd return to school after being in New York, I was bursting with excitement over what I had been able to experience and see, but my friends didn't seem interested, not even slightly. It was the strangest thing. They knew I had been away and they knew why, and we had decently close relationships, but nobody asked *anything* about what had happened while I was in the city.

It's not that I was looking to drone on and on about my days in New York, but I would have loved to have the chance to share a few highlights. A detail or two, maybe. At the time, work in the fashion industry was one of the biggest dreams in my heart, so I thought my friends would've cared enough to show some interest in it. They didn't even have to *be* interested in Fashion Week, but if they cared about me, couldn't they manage to at least *seem* interested?

Actually, no. Each time, no one asked a single question. And rather than force the awkward moment—"*Sooooo, Fashion Week was great . . .*"—I simply stayed quiet about my experiences and stayed confused about my friends' apparent disinterest. Without any outlet, the fresh bursts of fashion energy that were pulsing in my veins eventually fizzled back to normal levels.

Looking back on those college years now, it's a safe bet that what I saw from my friends was simply unintended exclusion. The people who were in my life were my real friends, and the fact that they didn't ask me about New York doesn't change that. Maybe they weren't sure what kinds of questions to ask, maybe they didn't feel knowledgeable enough about fashion, or maybe there was even some jealousy that played in. (After all, I basically got to miss class so I could go to some great East Coast parties.)

Regardless of what they intended, though, the result was the same. In my relationships with those friends, an entire corner of my life was overlooked and disregarded. It felt exclusive, because it *was* exclusive: My time at Fashion Week was excluded from our friendships completely. Which is perhaps another way of saying that a significant part of me wasn't made welcome in the relationship. Although I felt like *I* was welcome, I also got the sense that my Fashion Week experiences weren't. And sometimes that led to mind games—*did* these friends accept me for me, or would they have preferred to have me without the Fashion Week piece?

It wasn't a great feeling.

Unfortunately, a story like this just scratches the surface of what it means to be excluded. Most of us have seen people excluded more than we'd like to admit. People refuse to make room at the lunch table. People ignore someone in conversation or look away while passing someone in a hallway. People talk about social events with others who aren't invited. People post photos on social media of parties that others didn't get the chance to attend.

Or maybe it's even worse. Maybe it's blatant ridicule or rejection. Maybe it's hurtful comments or sneering looks. Maybe it's a total refusal to let conversation happen.

It's a disgusting scenario every time. And if you know the basic story of God's love for his people, you should understand why.

A Welcome for Outsiders

In Genesis, God tells one of his peoples' early ancestors to do something—*ahem*—interesting. The ancestor in this passage is Abraham, and by the time we get to him in chapter 17, God has already chosen him to be the starting point for what will one day become the whole nation of Israel. God even tells Abraham so, promising him that he'll have descendants as numerous as the stars.[71] God also vows that Abraham's children will one day have a land of their own. To assure Abraham about the land, God solidifies his promise to Abraham through a type of agreement known as a covenant.

We've mentioned God's covenant with Abraham already, in chapter 14 of this book, and we're going to take a closer look at it here. Having a familiarity with this covenant is important. It was a vastly significant theme in the Old Testament and a vital thread in the love story God was weaving for his people.

Many people think a covenant was the same thing as a promise, but a covenant had different implications. Specifically, it was a legal agreement that was made in the context of a relationship. In other words, it wasn't just two parties committing to something with words, then moving on from there. Through a covenant, two parties tied themselves together with an agreed-upon purpose.

Marriages were made through covenants. A king would covenant with a commoner under a protection/service covenant: The king would protect the commoner with his armies and his city walls, and the commoner would serve the king or pay a tax of sorts to the king. In the covenant, the lives on both sides became linked. That was central to the deal.

God's covenant with Abraham is unique in more than one way, but we're going to focus on just one here: God makes his covenant and then seemingly goes beyond it. What does that mean? Well, God specifies in Genesis 17 that his covenant with Abraham will pass down through Isaac, a son who will be born to Abraham and his wife, Sarah.[72] This is a necessary distinction because Abraham has another son, Ishmael, whose mother is Sarah's servant. Essentially, God is saying that Isaac, not Ishmael, will be the son of the covenant.

But that's not the full story. Beginning in Genesis 17:9, God informs Abraham what his responsibility in their covenant will be. God has already told Abraham what God's side of the covenant is: that he's going to bless Abraham and his descendants, he's going to make their numbers great, he's going to let them be his people, and he's going to be their God forever. As for Abraham's responsibility, what he needs to do is wear a sign of the covenant on his body. Along with all the other men of his household, he must be circumcised: A particular piece of his skin must be sliced off as a mark of the unending link between this family and God.

Aside from the fact that circumcision might seem like an odd way to signal a covenant, there's one part of this deal that's stranger still. When God tells Abraham who in his family needs to be circumcised, it's more than just Abraham and Isaac. No, God makes a point to include the male servants in Abraham's household, both those native to the land and foreign-born servants. "Your bodies will bear the mark of my everlasting covenant," God tells Abraham.[73] All of them. It was a wildly radical idea at the time.

Abraham and his servants lived in a time and place where there was a huge divide between two camps: (1) family and (2) everybody else. People were identified primarily by their clans and tribes—this meant that if you came from a foreign place or came from a family with a different bloodline, you were more or less an outsider. You could expect to be excluded from pretty much everything.

In this era, it wouldn't have surprised Abraham or anybody else that God promised to confirm their covenant through Isaac, because only Isaac would be the son of Abraham's wife. He'd have the "right" bloodline, through and through, whereas Ishmael wouldn't. So there would've been no surprise there. But it probably would have shocked Abraham that God would make a way for foreigners and nonfamily members to be included in this deal.

Something remarkable was going on. Do you see it? Isaac, the covenant son and the carrier of the promised bloodline for the future nation of Israel, hadn't even been born yet—and already God was messing with Abraham's understanding of how this covenant was going to work. By including foreigners and nonfamily members in his everlasting deal, God was sending a message loud and clear: *My generosity is not just for the insiders. With me the outsiders are just as welcome. The excluded ones, the ones nobody even thinks to take seriously—I see them, love them, and want them to be mine.*

Throughout the Bible, this message continues to

sound. While God keeps his Old Testament covenant with the nation of Israel in distinct ways, he is constantly extending it also to outsiders. The pattern culminates in the New Testament when, after the death of Jesus, Jews (Isaac's descendants) and Gentiles (everybody else) are now called "the same." Why? The apostle Paul says it's because "they have the same Lord, who gives generously to all who call on him."[74]

When we draw social boundary lines or allow ourselves to be drawn into cliques that include only some people and exclude the rest, we are denying a central piece of our loving God's good news. When we leave people out rather than drawing them in, we give no evidence of God's generous work in us. His love is big enough to redeem even sinful people—people who are and who deserve to be outsiders forever: you and me. And if his love is big enough to save *us*, then his love in us should be big enough to help us care for and welcome everybody else.

> *A beautiful heart cares for and*
> *welcomes everyone.*

Discussion Starters

1. Have you ever excluded someone else or gone along with excluding someone else? Why? What kept you from standing up for that person?

2. In the time of Abraham and Isaac, what was so remarkable about how God's covenant worked? What does that say about God?

3. What does it mean that we all deserve to be outsiders because of our sinfulness? Since we've been given God's acceptance anyway, how should that change the way we think about including others?

Part Six

Your Heart Looking Forward

GOD IS ALWAYS WILLING TO DO

WHATEVER'S NECESSARY

TO GET HIS PEOPLE BACK ON TRACK.

28

A *Heart* That Trusts

**Those Bored Months:
A Planning Story**

There are times when your plan works, and there are times when your plan falls flat. This section of time fits into the second category.

I had just graduated from college and was living at home, trying to get a job here in Dallas. Most of my peers were still away at college, including Brittany and another close friend of mine, who were studying abroad. There were good things in my life, like Steps (the program at my church) and extra time with my mom and dad, but nearly everything else seemed lackluster.

My main activity was scouring employee-wanted postings. I had found one position I was *really* interested in, an editorial job that was stationed locally. It seemed perfect, so I applied for it. I was so confident about this being the right fit for me, that when the company called to

schedule an interview, I thought, *Of course they're calling. This job is mine!*

It wasn't an arrogant thing; I simply felt certain that this must be what God had in store for me next. There weren't any other exciting options available, and I was sure I was ready to start my career. This *must* be it, because God wouldn't want me to sit around and get bored, would he? I went to the interview, and I absolutely nailed it. I was so excited afterward—this was really happening!

But they hired someone else, just like I had thought they wouldn't.

I got bored, just like I had thought I shouldn't.

Man. Here I was, just out of college—I wanted to feel like I was on the brink of something phenomenal, but most days I simply felt out of the loop and stuck in a rut. I didn't understand how that could be what God wanted for me. How was it at all useful to him for me to be sitting around doing nothing?

I asked that question a lot during those months. And every time I asked it, I was demonstrating just how short-sighted and circumstance-focused and self-centered I can be. I was looking at God, sure, but I was looking at him through a lens of what *I* thought was important and what was directly in front of *me*. I didn't much consider what he was doing in others' lives or how my own circumstances were just one tiny piece of the grand good-news story that he was writing all over the universe.

One more thing I didn't consider: that compared to my own plan for my life, God's plan might be worlds and worlds bigger, not to mention endlessly more glorious.

While I restlessly searched for more available jobs in my field, I figured I might as well use some of my free time

to dig deeply into the Steps program. I've already mentioned how much God used it in me—transforming how I understood him, revealing destructive patterns in my relationships and in my way of thinking, and helping me forgive myself for poor choices I had made in the past. Still, as I studied and confessed and prayed my way through the program, I found that even Steps was in some ways increasing my impatience about the other parts of my life. It was such an odd combination, feeling so enlivened and at the same time so aimless. Here I was, learning, getting stronger, and becoming more dependent on God—why didn't it seem like he was using me?

Again, the answer was clouded by my limited perspective. It had never crossed my mind that God was slowing down my life in order to prepare me for something bigger and harder than I could've ever imagined. All I saw was the progress that I had made already; what I didn't see and couldn't have seen was the sort of fresh wisdom, strength, and dependence I would need in just a few short months. Only God could see that. Only he knew the ways he was going to use me for his purposes—not only in Dallas, not only in editorial work, and not only in my existing relationships, but far beyond.

There I was, thinking it would be amazing to land a job at a magazine in Dallas, and it would've been. But God was looking further down the road, and he was looking at different venues. He had opportunities for me that I wouldn't have thought would be available—certainly not within a year or so, and probably not ever. God wanted me to share his love and represent his Kingdom on a national and even a worldwide scale. His opportunities for me were to be a correspondent for *E! News* and a guest on *Today*, for starters. And every bit as important as things like that, he wanted to accomplish a thorough overhaul of my heart, not just a "good enough" one.

He wanted to make me a more willing and more faithful servant to him, and he was making it possible for that to happen, no matter how confused I got about it. Only God knew how much of a break it would take for me to absorb what he needed me to learn, especially with me dragging my feet all the way.

Getting Things Really, Really Wrong

Probably one of the top ten most well-known people in the Bible is the apostle Paul. One of the earliest converts to Christianity, he was used by God to lead and disciple many of the first Christian churches that gathered outside Jerusalem. He visited the churches regularly and expressed God's love to them through letters, and a portion of those letters now make up a big chunk of the New Testament. Romans, Galatians, Ephesians, Colossians, Philippians, Titus—all these books and more were written by Paul.

Paul was a brilliant scholar and a gifted teacher. He was bold, wise, and diligent. We can see from all his writings that he was faithful to God's work. His confidence in God enabled him to endure a number of intense trials during his ministry: beatings by the Romans, a shipwreck, and imprisonment, to name just a few. But even in the life of Paul we see how a God-seeking and well-meaning person can miss the point of things.

Before Paul became a Christian and even before his name was Paul (he used to be called Saul), he was one of the Jewish leaders in Jerusalem. As he explained to the Philippians later:

I was a member of the Pharisees, who demand the strictest obedience to the Jewish law. . . . And as for righteousness, I obeyed the law without fault.[75]

Here was a man who knew the Scriptures—that's what the Jewish law was, at the time. In fact, Saul knew the Scriptures so well and was so devoted to them that he was able to claim that he obeyed them "without fault." Despite all this, though, Saul didn't recognize the Messiah when he came into the world. Worse than that, Saul thought Jesus was a phony and a heretic.

Almost as soon as the Bible begins talking about the Christian church, it also begins talking about the ways Saul persecuted the church. In Acts 7 and 8, we see Saul giving approval to the stoning death of Stephen who, with his face "as bright as an angel's,"[76] had professed to the Jewish council why he believed Jesus was the Messiah. Immediately after this, we read that "Saul was going everywhere to destroy the church. He went from house to house, dragging out both men and women to throw them into prison."[77] A chapter later, we find him "uttering threats with every breath . . . eager to kill the Lord's followers."[78]

Saul was doing all these things because of God—or so he thought. After studying the Scriptures and devoting his whole life to them, he believed with all that was in him that Christians needed to be dragged from their homes, imprisoned, and killed. He was certain that Jesus had been full of lies and that now Jesus' followers were too, and he was clearly willing to do whatever it took to stop them.

Next up for Saul, he began making his way toward the city of Damascus, where he planned to arrest all the Christians he could find. He had even sought out the Jewish high priest and gotten his official endorsement for the job. But right in the middle of this self-appointed "seek and destroy" mission, something stopped Saul. Some*one* stopped him.

> As he was approaching Damascus on this mission, a light from heaven suddenly shone down around him. He fell to the ground and heard a voice saying to him, "Saul! Saul! Why are you persecuting me?"
>
> "Who are you, lord?" Saul asked.
>
> And the voice replied, "I am Jesus, the one you are persecuting! Now get up and go into the city, and you will be told what you must do."[79]

Saul obeyed. While he was in Damascus, God (through a vision) visited a Christian named Ananias and told him to go to Saul. Ananias initially protested because he had heard of Saul and the way Saul persecuted Christians.

> But the Lord said, "Go, for Saul is my chosen instrument to take my message to the Gentiles and to kings, as well as to the people of Israel. And I will show him how much he must suffer for my name's sake."[80]

That's how Saul's plans for his life changed. They collided with God's plans for him, which went in a completely different direction from where Saul expected them to take him. Even though he seemed to think he was chasing after God's Word as zealously as possible, he was way off course. Thankfully, God is always willing to do what's necessary to get his people on track and set straight.

You might have some idea of where you think your life

is headed. Consider this: You are not God, so your plans are probably wrong on some counts. Maybe they're wrong on most counts. There are things God wants to do in and through you that might never show up on your radar, apart from him. He will keep you away from some opportunities you want, and he will fling you headfirst (it'll feel that way sometimes, at least) into circumstances that you don't want. But if you're willing to trust him along the way, you'll be able to look for and find his glory in all of it. And if you're willing to find his glory in it, you'll be able to trust him in his plan.

A beautiful heart trusts God's plan, even
when it doesn't seem to make sense.

Discussion Starters

1. Have you ever seen your own plans for your life fall flat? When and how? Has God taught you something through that experience? If not, what do you think you could still learn from him because of it?

2. Read Acts 9:10-19. What was Saul doing before Ananias went to visit him? What do you think we can learn from this?

3. Do you trust God's plan for your life? Are you more interested in his glory than you are in your own plans? If not, how do you think that it would help to find his glory in them?

WHEN WE
EXPERIENCE
FEAR, WE
CAN LOOK TO
GOD FOR OUR
BRAVERY AND
BOLDNESS.

29

A *Heart* That Fears

Four Plus Four:
An Errand-Running Story

It was a day marked with fear. That's what I remember most about the start of it.

I was still early in my recovery process, still spending a lot of time trying to deal with the effects of my accident, and I woke up one morning in an especially bad place emotionally. There were four fears that had been on my mind for days, and I couldn't seem to shake them. They were practically all I could think about, every day from beginning to end.

One, I was afraid that I wasn't going to be able to handle the suffering in my life well. Two, I was afraid that I would never be able to hold a child. Three, I was afraid about how people would respond to my changed appearance. Four—well, we'll get to number four in a little while.

As it happened, I had to run errands at four places

that day. I had to go to training, to two different grocery stores, and to Ulta (a cosmetic store). There was no leaving my fears behind, so I carried them with me alongside my gym bag, and I took off to tackle the day as best I could. I didn't have high hopes about it.

After training, though, a woman stopped me in the parking lot.

"Wait!" she said. "I just have to say this to you." She told me that she had heard about my accident soon after it happened and had been praying for me ever since. "And I actually have a pretty bad case of breast cancer," she said, "and your story has helped me know that I can pull through this. It has brought me so much encouragement!"

There I was, afraid about my own suffering despite being on the upswing physically, and here was this woman, with the outcome of her cancer treatment still uncertain, talking to me about encouragement. Taking time to encourage *me*.

Next on my errand list was grocery store number one, where another woman noticed me and told me her sister had been born with only one hand.

"Really?" I replied. "Does she have any children? I've been trying to figure out if I could ever hold a child."

"She has three."

The woman gave me her sister's contact information so I could call with any questions I might have.

Next, at Ulta, a woman approached me and said that my pastor and friend, Matt, had recently preached at her church. She said Matt had told some of my story, and it had connected with her because her son had also been in a terrible accident. The woman described a little bit of what he had been through, and it sounded worlds more difficult

than what I had been facing. The physical changes that he had endured were far more extensive and obvious than mine. At the same time, when she talked about him, he sounded like such a cool person, with an amazingly bright outlook and a strong resolve. It made me think twice about my own physical changes, no question.

The fourth errand I ran was to grocery store number two. Something reassuring happened there too, and like the other three instances of the day, this one matched perfectly to one of the four fears I had been unable to overcome. I remember going home, being in awe about how each of those fears had been addressed explicitly. I remember being *so* changed in my spirit that day. But for the life of me, I can't remember what happened on my fourth errand.

In part that's because the fourth fear, like the three others, had been rattling me for days—I don't remember *it* anymore either. I have zero recollection of what it was.

How can that be? It's because God, through his mighty love (including tangible interactions in parking lots and grocery stores), can take fear so far away that it is actually and completely gone.

The Good Kind of Fear

The Bible talks about fear a lot, but the way it talks about fear could seem confusing at first. That's because sometimes it tells us *not* to fear, and sometimes it tells us *to* fear. Based on that alone, it's easy to wonder: Is fear a bad thing or a good thing? Should we fear or not?

But in paying attention to a few different kinds of Bible verses about fear, we can see that God's Word makes a clear distinction between bad and good fear. In the Bible, fear is a good thing when it's a proper fear of the Lord. Proverbs 1, for example, says, "Fear of the LORD is the foundation of true knowledge."[81] In the Gospel of Luke it says, "[God] shows mercy from generation to generation to all who fear him."[82] There are plenty of verses like this, illustrating the good kind of fear.

In contrast, fear is shown as a bad thing in the Bible too. Specifically, it's a bad thing when it's directed toward something or someone other than God. Psalm 23 tells us not to fear evil, for instance. And angels, when they appear in the Bible, seem to constantly be telling people to "Fear not!"

Why should we fear God? And why should we fear God but *not* other things, not even angels? To answer those questions, let's take a closer look at fear.

Here's a simple definition: Fear is the emotion that emerges when we see that something or someone else is stronger than we are. More specifically: Fear is what we feel when we're aware that we could be overpowered. That's why typically we have a hard time thinking of fear as a good thing. (When is being overpowered a pleasant experience?)

Looking at this emotion through that lens, we can see that fear is a perfectly fitting way to feel in response to God. He is stronger than us, after all. He's so strong that, if he wanted to, he could overpower us in the worst, most painful way: condemnation. In his purity, God has every right to look at our sin and banish us to hell half a heartbeat later.

Fear God? Oh, yes. We would be wrong *not* to be terrified, on some level, by who God is and what he can do.

There's a catch to that, though. God's power to condemn us represents only *part* of his power, so if we fear him only for that, we miss seeing the big picture. We miss

seeing God's greatest strength. That's because although God's power to condemn us is strong, his power to rescue us is even stronger.

Through Jesus' death on the cross, God created a way for love and mercy, not punishment, to be his response to our sin. We've talked about this before, but it's worth repeating: Jesus took the punishment so we could have that love. Although our sinfulness deserves death, in Christ we're given life—and not just any life, but eternal life with the One who loves us most. We're given acceptance, freedom, joy, and so much more.

Sometimes we're even given—at a grocery store, at the gym, in a parking lot—tiny, tailor-made reminders from him that he sees where we hurt and knows our worldly fears. His love is potent enough to boost us in ways that are *that* specific and obvious.

When we glimpse God's love and begin to fear it, understanding how powerful it is, our other fears shrink and fade by comparison. This is why God can tell us to *not* fear other things. It's because nothing else seems powerful when it's stacked up next to God's love and forgiveness. When we've been given his gift of redemption, there's no shadow that can ultimately darken us. There is nothing more to fear.

In the Bible, when people are fearful of their circumstances, often what we see is that God boosts their courage by reminding them about himself. For instance, Isaiah delivers God's words: "Fear not, for I have redeemed you; I have called you by name, you are mine."[83] Or in Genesis, God says: "Do not be afraid, Abram, for I will protect you."[84]

Similarly, when we experience fearful thoughts about our circumstances, we can look to God for our bravery and boldness. We can be overpowered by his love, remembering that he has conquered our biggest threat, eternal death, and has defeated our one truly vicious foe, sin. Because of that, under God's leading, we can stand confidently in the face of any danger. What can this world do to us that would tarnish his love and redemption? What could anyone or anything ever take away from his mighty generosity toward us?

> *Can anything ever separate us from Christ's love? Does it mean he no longer loves us if we have trouble or calamity, or are persecuted, or hungry, or destitute, or in danger, or threatened with death? . . . No, despite all these things, overwhelming victory is ours through Christ, who loved us.*
>
> *And I am convinced that nothing can ever separate us from God's love. Neither death nor life, neither angels nor demons, neither our fears for today nor our worries about tomorrow—not even the powers of hell can separate us from God's love. No power in the sky above or in the earth below—indeed, nothing in all creation will ever be able to separate us from the love of God that is revealed in Christ Jesus our Lord.*
>
> ROMANS 8:35, 37-39

A beautiful heart fears God, acknowledging that his power is the greatest.

Discussion Starters

1. "Typically we have a hard time thinking of fear as a good thing." Why?

2. According to the Bible, what kinds of fears are bad fears? Why does this make sense, given what we know about God?

3. What circumstances, people, or things are most likely to make you afraid? How should fearing the Lord affect that?

"Here on earth
you will have
many trials
and sorrows.
But take heart,
because I have
overcome the world."
John 16:33

30

A *Heart* That Hopes

Darts on a Life's Map:
An Everybody Story

From 1998 to 2004, a *CBS News* correspondent named Steve Hartman traveled the United States finding stories based on what a dartboard and phone books told him. Inspired by a local news reporter who had a similar system but used only a phone book, Steve took the idea to a national scale by adding the dartboard. Initially, he tried it as a joke—until he realized it actually worked. That's how "Everybody Has a Story" was born.

The idea was simple. It began with throwing a dart at a map of the United States. The thrower would throw backward and over a shoulder, to keep from aiming anywhere—wherever the dart landed determined the city, town, or county where Steve was headed next. He'd hop on a plane or in a car, depending on how far he'd be going, and he would get himself to that one point on the map. There, he'd find a phone book.

Riffling through the pages—again, not looking—Steve would randomly point one finger onto a single page. Whatever phone number he was pointing to (assuming whoever picked up the phone agreed to it) would be where he'd go for his next TV story.

He'd interview the person, and typically within the first day, Steve would zero in on the story he should tell. They'd spend the next day filming in order to get everything they'd need for a prime-time TV slot. At the end of it, the subject of Steve's current story would throw a dart at his US map, leading to the next assignment.

Steve's efforts to find and tell untold stories were popular for the entire six years they were on the air. Viewers loved the idea that anybody, *anybody*, had a compelling life full of experiences, motives, and memories that could make your heart break. The title was true: Everybody has a story—and they all seemed to be worth watching. People faithfully tuned in to the series until it ended, when Steve was promoted to another position at CBS.[85]

I think it's fair to suggest a slight change to this idea and say instead that *everybody has a struggle*. You, me, every person we care about, and every person we meet—each of us has a struggle. For me, the struggle lately has been my recovery and healing. But there were struggles before that too. In the time leading up to my accident, my struggle was trying to figure out where God was leading me. Before that, it was learning to know God and submit to him. Before that, it was my parents' divorce and separation. If you could throw a dart at a map of my life or your life or anyone else's, every hit could be a bull's-eye on some kind of struggle or another.

There is no shortage of pain and difficulty in this

world, no matter who you are, where you're from, or what you believe. And perhaps it's necessary to emphasize this in another way: Belonging to God doesn't make a person one bit immune to the effects and problems of a sinful world. Jesus told his followers that God doesn't play favorites—using an agricultural reference, he says that his father "gives his sunlight to both the evil and the good, and he sends rain on the just and the unjust alike."[86] God is generous to everyone. But that doesn't mean that storms, damaging winds, and disasters are out of the question. Jesus explicitly tells us to plan on the bad stuff too: "Here on earth you will have many trials and sorrows."[87] He couldn't be more direct, could he?

Everybody has a struggle. Everybody should expect to have many struggles. That's reality, no matter who you are. So the only question that's individual to a person is this: How do your struggles impact you?

Struggles can either make us stronger or make us shrink into weakness. The difference between the two is, as usual, a matter of deciding whether to accept or reject God's good news.

Pain as a Signal

I love working out and being active. I always have. Because of that, one of the upsides of my recovery process has been that it requires me to go to the gym regularly. I work out with a special trainer, Sheri, a couple of days a week in order to keep my arm muscles strong and functioning, to keep my mind and memory flexed, and to focus on overall fitness.

Sheri is an expert at what she does, and the company she works for, Athletes' Performance (AP), specializes in training elite athletes. When my family and I first heard about Sheri, we thought there was no chance I'd ever get to train with her. But when we called, she miraculously had an opening on her schedule!

On any given day at AP, some athletes are working to stay in shape during their sport's off-season, some are trying to rebuild strength and ability after a surgery or an injury, and some are seeking that extra edge that will help them advance to a professional level. Some people might think it would be glamorous to be surrounded by people like this. It's not. It's a gym. It's full of grunting, grimacing, sweating, straining, and pain. But given the caliber of the athletes who are there, it's safe to say that the pain at AP is different from the pain that happens at other gyms. It's more focused, more specific, and simply *more*.

Any physical trainer will tell you that pain is the key to strength. When you work out or do something active, if you feel pain in your muscles later, often that pain is signaling that there are tiny tears in the fibers of your muscles. Give it a few days of rest, and the pain will be gone because the tears will have healed. Here's the amazing part: Having healed, those muscles are actually stronger than they were before.

Skilled trainers and athletes work to capitalize on the way our bodies naturally build strength. They design workouts that will lead to the right kinds of muscle tearing in the right places and at the right times. It's a delicate balance, to build and maintain strength without pushing too far and causing injury. But when it's done well and continually over a period of time, it can increase a person's power and stamina like crazy, athlete or not.

But . . .

There's a big difference between physical training and spiritual training. In proper physical training, pain is the *result* of a good workout. In spiritual training, pain is the *signal* that a workout should begin. When we're struggling with something, dealing with a problem, facing a fear, or going through a tough spot, that pain is telling us to dig in for some spiritual strengthening.

The book of Romans puts it this way:

> Christ has brought us into this place of undeserved privilege where we now stand, and we confidently and joyfully look forward to sharing God's glory.
>
> We can rejoice, too, when we run into problems and trials, for we know that they help us develop endurance. And endurance develops strength of character, and character strengthens our confident hope of salvation. And this hope will not lead to disappointment. For we know how dearly God loves us, because he has given us the Holy Spirit to fill our hearts with his love.[88]

There's a whole lot of content in that one little passage, but it's pretty straightforward when you break it down into pieces. If it were a sports manual, it might read like this: Practice hard, and it will produce good game-day stats. Lots of good game-day stats make you a dependably good player. Being a dependably good player makes people want you on their team. Then you won't have to wonder if you're going to be put in for the game, because with your record, that's what makes sense.

Now, here's one way to restate the passage in biblical terms: If you've been rescued by Jesus, then struggles in life force you to get through them by being strong in the Lord. Being strong in the Lord over and over is evidence of a pattern of strength in the Lord. That pattern helps give confidence that your faith in God is real—proof that his redemption really has happened in your life. In that case, you have every reason to believe that one day you will share in his glory. This is your hope: You know God's love and have seen it fill you.

Here's the thing. I couldn't be happier about the fact that, with God's love surrounding me, I've been able to get through the trauma of a major accident and the long recovery that has followed. I'm overjoyed, knowing that by God's grace I've been able to show some strength in him and even build some more. But this whole ordeal has been just one struggle, one period of struggle, on my personal lifelong map of struggles. There's no telling what trial the dart will land on next. Not for me, not for you, not for anybody.

Years from now I don't want to be pointing to only an accident and a recovery as evidence of God's work in my life. As time goes on, I know I'll face more and different trials, just like everybody will. And I want to find strength in the Lord for them too. I want his strength to be my pattern, come what may.

I want to be able to look back at my life and know that I trusted him over and over and over, because his love had proved to me that he would be faithful and faithful and faithful again. I want my faith muscles to be trained for action so that when pain and struggles come, my instant response is to bring them to God.

Wouldn't it be incredible to build a history of perseverance like that? Think of how wonderful it would feel to wear God's strength like an old familiar hat—one we've put on so often that now we grab for it almost without realizing it. One that fits comfortably and is practically a natural extension of us because it's been worn so much. One that reminds us and shows the world that loving God is not just something to talk about. When the rubber meets the road, God's love is actual living-and-breathing hope.

A beautiful heart has hope through struggles and suffering, knowing they build strength in the Lord.

Discussion Starters

1. If it's true that "everyone has a struggle," what's yours right now? What's the hardest or most painful part of your current struggle?

2. What does it mean that in spiritual training, pain is a signal? Do you react to trials and struggles in this way?

3. What's so great about perseverance? Why should we want to consistently rely on God's strength in our struggles? How do you think you can begin doing that or keep doing that today?

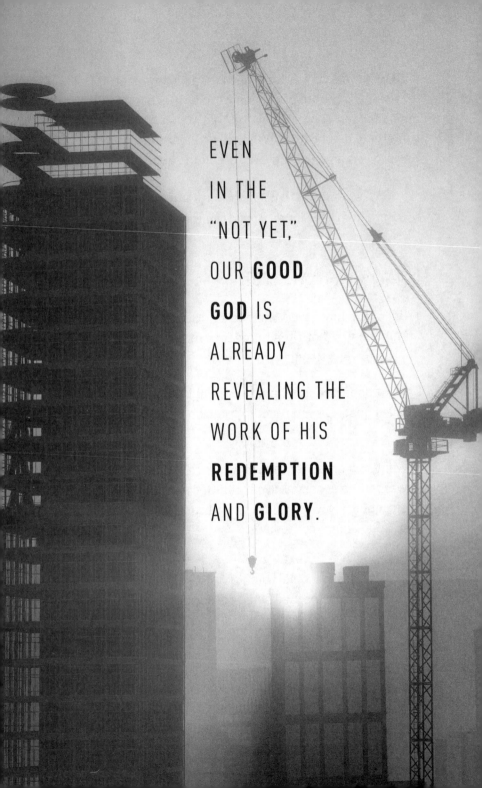

EVEN IN THE "NOT YET," OUR **GOOD GOD** IS ALREADY REVEALING THE WORK OF HIS **REDEMPTION** AND **GLORY**.

31

A *Heart* That Waits

The Drive-By Meltdown: A Wedding Story

A flowing bridesmaid gown, a stunning bouquet, a fancy limousine—then, unexpectedly, a particular scene outside the window, and I nearly lost it.

My friend Caroline had just gotten married, and along with the rest of the bridal party, I was riding with a group from the ceremony to the reception. The mood was light and celebratory, like it should've been. And maybe it would've stayed that way, had I realized a little sooner where we were heading. I didn't.

Months had passed since my accident. My major surgeries were long over; I was living on my own again; and with the help of family, friends, medical professionals, and strangers, I had been fortunate to make great strides in recovery. It was a sheer delight for me to be able to take part in other people's lives once again, especially on days

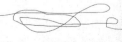

like this. Caroline was one of my longtime friends, and I couldn't have been happier for her. I had planned on the day being nothing but beautiful.

Then, for the first time since my accident, I was looking at the airport where the accident had happened.

We were simply driving by—no big deal, right? But that sight triggered something in me, and in the midst of the day's joyous emotions and happy moments, suddenly I was a ball of nerves, frenzied tears, and rapidly smearing mascara. I didn't know how to stop the reaction, and I wasn't entirely sure how it had begun in the first place. I think the not knowing was the scariest and oddest part about it.

There are other things too. I still struggle with the thought of being seen in public or by acquaintances without my prosthetic arm. My counselor tells me this is normal because it can take years for a person's brain to process a traumatic change to the body. But for some reason I have a hard time letting myself respond normally to this. I want to stop dreading the moments when new people might see my left arm for what it is. I want to stop being surprised when, standing in front of a dressing-room mirror, still expecting to see two hands on my body, I turn around and see only one instead. I want all this processing to be finished.

But it isn't. Maybe it won't be for a while. And you know what? That doesn't have to be entirely a bad thing.

Already and Not Yet

In Old Testament times, animal sacrifices were central to worship. This might sound cold or ruthless, but it wasn't. The sacrificial system was something that God had given the Hebrew people as a reminder that he loved them and would forgive them of their sins.

It was a reminder, too, that the proper payment for a sinful heart was a serious one: blood.

Judaism required sacrifices on a regular basis for all kinds of things. There was a daily sacrifice in the Temple, made on behalf of all the people for their sin; along with that, there were sacrifices made to atone for individual sins, sacrifices for restoring a person's relationship with God after a sin was committed, sacrifices to signify true repentance, and even sacrifices for sins that had been committed unknowingly.

There was also a day set aside annually for a special sacrifice. This day was the biggest sacrificing day of the year. It was called Yom Kippur, which means "Day of Atonement," and it centered on two goats. Every Yom Kippur, a priest took two spotless goats from among the Israelites' flocks. After basically drawing straws for what happened to which goat, the priest would sacrifice one of the goats on an altar. The people understood that that first spotless goat's blood was paying for their sins. That year, that one goat signified that they wouldn't have to die for their own sin. The goat had taken their place.

Then there was the second spotless goat. The priest took this goat and, putting his hands on its head, confessed all of Israel's sins onto the goat. This symbolized a transfer of the sins: All the ways that Israel had sinned against God were now carried on that one little goat's head. (You almost have to wonder if it had a hard time walking afterward.)

The second goat's job was to carry all of Israel's sins out from among them. *Far* out. The goat was led away to the wilderness and abandoned there.[89] What this goat signified was that the Israelites' sins couldn't stick with them after the first goat's sacrifice. The sins were completely gone, forever. (This is how the word *scapegoat* came to be.)

Year after year, the goats gave quite a picture of God's forgiving love. Just imagine seeing the blood of the one on the altar or watching the other leave town, and knowing what it all meant!

Still, it was an incomplete picture because there is only so much that two little goats could do. Goats are goats, and people are people—and not even the blood of a perfectly spotless goat will fully cover the sin of a person. The forgiveness bought by Israel's many animal sacrifices would always have limits. The goats would carry the weight and punishment of sin for just one year at a time.

So every year, two new goats were necessary. And every year, it was a picture of how God loved his people *and* a picture of how the story wasn't yet fully told. That's because complete and lasting forgiveness hadn't arrived—for that, the people were still waiting. The universe was waiting.

Forgiveness was here *already*, and also *not yet*.

One day, the whole problem of sin would have its full solution. The Israelites' system of animal sacrifices was just the opening act for something bigger. As the book of Hebrews explains, in Jesus, the perfect sacrifice arrived.[90] His death would pour blood on God's altar once and for all. Taking our sins upon himself, he would carry them away forever.

And even with that, we are still waiting in a way. The story still isn't fully told. Although the price of our sin has already been paid, we still live in a world marked by sin.

Sin has been crushed already, and also not yet. We still see its effects and are impacted deeply by them. All of us long for a day when the wrongs caused by sin are eliminated, when everything that happens is only and always right and good.

Romans 8 says that all of creation is groaning, like a woman in labor, for that day. When it finally comes, creation will no longer be chained by death and decay. It will be free. And there's more:

> *We believers also groan, even though we have the Holy Spirit within us as a foretaste of future glory, for we long for our bodies to be released from sin and suffering. We, too, wait with eager hope for the day when God will give us our full rights as his adopted children, including the new bodies he has promised us. We were given this hope when we were saved.*[91]

As unthinkably wonderful as it is that Jesus came and died for us, and as magnificent as it is that he took the punishment for our sin, even *that* is like two little goats compared to what's still coming, which is total glory. Yes, it gets unimaginably better than even this.

One day, Jesus will return for his people, and then all our heavy weights will be lifted. All our wounds will disappear, as if they never existed, not even for a moment. (Do you see!? It says *new bodies!*) God, who has already made it possible for us to stand before him and be seen as righteous, will take care of the one detail that hasn't happened yet: He'll put sin in its place forever, and he'll rescue his people from every single trace of it.

There will be no reason for crying, ever again. We will not be confused. We will not feel lost or afraid or alone. Our insecurities will be gone for good. We will no longer doubt God's love for us, we will no longer wonder if he really is good, we will no longer fear that he's on a power trip or that he's going to abandon us or use us. We won't seek acceptance because we'll know his acceptance perfectly, as much as it can possibly be known. Everything in God's heavens and earth—including us—will be fully alive and beautiful, all the time. There will be no question about that. Hurts won't happen anymore. Death will be done.

That's what it will be like to experience God's presence fully. That's what's coming our way.

It's not here yet. Some days it can almost seem like it might never arrive. But we can count on it and be glad in the midst of our waiting, because even in the "not yet," our good God is already revealing the work of his redemption and glory. Even now, with our vision clouded by sinfulness, we can see it. And he has told us that the view will only get better.

A beautiful heart is thankful for the forgiveness
that has already come and waits eagerly
for the glory that hasn't yet appeared.

Discussion Starters

1. In the Old Testament, the Israelites sacrificed animals. What did that signify about God's love for them? How did Jesus' death demonstrate God's love to an even fuller extent?

2. What does it mean to live both in the "already" and the "not yet"? What has God given us already, and what has he promised that hasn't happened yet?

3. What's one way that you can remember to be thankful for the "already"? How can that thankfulness change the way you think about the "not yet"?

Epilogue

Of all the things that have happened in my life, easily the most significant one is that God has shown me that he loves me in spite of my sin. He has forgiven me even though I deserve punishment for the ways my sin hurts him. I am loved *that much*! There is nothing more beautiful in my life or anyone else's.

You've made it all the way through this book, and I hope that by now you understand (or are beginning to understand) what real beauty is. I hope you see that God's love is the one thing that is spellbindingly beautiful. I hope it is captivating you. I hope you long for it to define you, for God's beauty to take root in your heart.

But there is only one way for it to define you, and that happens through accepting his love. Putting his love at the center of you. What does that mean? It's as simple as this: Admit to God that you know you don't deserve his forgiveness, and accept the generous forgiveness that he gives. Tell him you understand that on your own you're unlovely and filled with ugly idols ruling (and ruining) your heart. Tell him that you want him to take over, so your heart can be healed and consumed by his beautiful love instead.

If you do that for the first time today, or if you've done that for the first time while reading this book, will you also do one more thing? Will you find a trusted Christian friend (preferably another female) to tell, and ask her to support you and pray for you as you begin this adventure? You have an exciting journey ahead of you, with plenty more beauty to be unfolded as you follow Jesus. You'll want to have others by your side to cheer you on and celebrate this new life with you.

On behalf of myself, the other young women reading this book, and a worldwide community of people who've all been changed by God's love, welcome to the family!

Acknowledgments

From Lauren:
I'm grateful to many people for helping *Your Beautiful Heart* come together, and I'd like to especially highlight some in particular. Tyndale House Publishers has demonstrated stellar efforts from beginning to end. Greg Johnson played a big role in conceiving the ideas for this book and helping steer it in the right direction. Lisa Velthouse partnered with me to shape the manuscript and articulate its message beautifully. My friends walked through this project with me faithfully, as they do with everything. My wonderful family, Jeff and Cheryl Scruggs and Shaun and Brittany Morgan, encouraged me and stood by me every step of the way. My fiancé, Jason Kennedy, contributed an amazing foreword, not to mention constant love and support. Thank you!

From Lisa:
It's always clear, from the inside of a book project, how much God did to make it come together. Every time I think of how God orchestrated this project, I'm amazed. Most notably on my end, he gave me the support I needed to complete the necessary work—thanks to a pregnancy and a husband who deployed unexpectedly, that was a far more challenging task than I had anticipated at the outset.

Thanks to Nathan, for your constant support, selflessness, feedback, and great ideas, and for doting on our toddler every weekend during the first-draft stage. Thank you for being a picture of God's love and gentleness to me.

Thanks to Krista, for your kindness and encouragement, your early-morning smiles, and your faithful, loving care for Miss C.

Thanks to two years' worth of community groups, for your prayers, your comic relief, and for being our family's California "home."

Thanks to Greg Johnson of WordServe Literary, for your consistent advocacy and for thinking of this partnership and making it happen.

Thanks to Jeff and Cheryl Scruggs for your hospitality, tenacity, and eagerness to tell a story in the best way possible.

Thanks to Chuckie and John for the two weeks of rescue and loving presence after the baby arrived.

Thanks to my parents, in-laws, and siblings for giving constantly and thoughtfully, and for keeping tabs on us when things get crazy.

Thanks to the team at Tyndale, and in particular Sarah, Kim, and Jillian, for your excellence paired with grace.

Thanks to everyone who in any way, large or small, helped our family survive the book-and-deployment-and-toddler-and-baby days. I'm thrilled to say there are too many of you to mention.

Thanks to Lauren, for your warmth, openness, encouragement, strength of faith, and hard work. God's love is plainly evident in your life, and collaborating with you has been a privilege and a delight.

Thanks to you, reader, for going on this journey with us. May you discover the beauty of God's Good News, and may it transform you from head to toe, from the inside out, for his glory.

About the Authors

$\mathcal{L}$ auren Scruggs is the founder and editor of *LOLO Magazine*, an online lifestyle hub that unites all things fashion, beauty, and health. Lauren was born in Redondo Beach and raised in Dallas, so you can call her a California girl whose roots are deep in the heart of Texas. Her love for fashion has been tightly sewn through her internship experience in the wardrobe department for CW's *Gossip Girl*, the Michael Kors showroom in New York City, and reporting for the New York, Paris, and Montreal Fashion Weeks. In February of 2013, Lauren covered the New York Fashion Week as the fashion correspondent for *E! News*. In addition, she is a regular Style Squad reporter on *The Broadcast* in Dallas and is currently collaborating with Outline the Sky in creating a "LOLO" T-shirt line. Lauren emcees specific fund-raising events for Texas Scottish Rite Hospital and Children's Hospital and enjoys hosting fashion events at Neiman Marcus and other stores.

Lauren's first book, *Still LoLo*, was published in 2012. Along with Bethany Hamilton, Lauren started a yearly retreat for girls who have lost a limb to create a community and encourage others on their journey. After discovering that insurance companies view prostheses as a luxury instead of a necessity, Lauren is in the process of starting a foundation with the intent to provide beautiful prostheses for many people in need.

$\mathcal{L}$ isa Velthouse is a freelance writer and speaker. The author and contributor of five books, including *Saving My First Kiss* and *Craving Grace*, she was also once the Brio Girl for *Brio* magazine. She's the wife to an active-duty Marine Corps infantry officer and the mom of two small children. Read Lisa's blog and find out more about her at LisaVelthouse.com.

Endnotes

1. From Isaiah 53:2-3
2. John 19:30
3. Judah Smith, a pastor in Seattle, makes this point beautifully in his book *Jesus Is: Find a New Way to Be Human* (Nashville: Thomas Nelson, 2013). I highly recommend it!
4. Romans 11:5-6
5. From Luke 23:39
6. From Luke 23:42-43
7. The "Lisa" here is Lisa Velthouse, my collaborator on this book.
8. Exodus 24:3
9. Exodus 20:3
10. Credit goes to Timothy Keller for this definition, which could be attributed to a number of his sermons and books.
11. Mark 2:5
12. Mark 2:8-12
13. I highly recommend this series—it's called The Gospel of Suffering by Tullian Tchividjian, and you can find it here: http://www.crpc.org /media/series/job:-the-gospel-of-suffering.
14. You can find God's challenge to Job in Job 38-41.
15. Job 3:1, 8
16. Job 3:12
17. Job 7:11
18. John 10:5, 27
19. Psalm 119:11
20. You can find this story in Acts 2.
21. Galatians 5:16
22. Psalm 13:1-2
23. Psalm 13:3-4
24. Psalm 13:5-6
25. John 4:23
26. Luke 15:14-24

27. The book *The Prodigal God* by Timothy Keller goes into much detail about this parable from Luke 15. Credit goes to Keller for some of the observations about the older son that are mentioned here.
28. 2 Samuel 12:5
29. 2 Samuel 12:7
30. 2 Samuel 12:13
31. Psalm 46:10
32. Psalm 46:10, NASB, emphasis added
33. Exodus 20:8
34. Genesis 1:28
35. Genesis 6:5
36. Genesis 9:1
37. See Genesis 17.
38. Exodus 19:5
39. 1 Corinthians 10:7
40. 1 Corinthians 10:8, 10
41. 1 Corinthians 10:21
42. Luke 18:13
43. 1 Kings 3:5
44. 1 Kings 3:6-8
45. 1 Kings 3:9
46. John 13:3-5
47. John 13:8
48. John 13:8
49. John 13:15
50. Luke 10: 41-42
51. You can find out more about WWP at WoundedWarriorProject.org.
52. Philippians 2:7-8
53. Philippians 2: 3-5
54. 1 John 4:19, 21
55. Romans 2:4
56. John 8:7
57. John 8:9-11
58. Ephesians 2:1-2a, 3
59. Ephesians 2:4-5a, 6-7
60. Ephesians 2:10
61. You can find this story in John 6:1-13.
62. In the wilderness with Moses, the miracle food that God's people ate was called manna. This is mentioned in John 6:31: "After all, our ancestors ate manna while they journeyed through the wilderness! The Scriptures say, 'Moses gave them bread from heaven to eat.'"
63. John 6:32-35
64. Bob Briner, *Roaring Lambs* (Grand Rapids: Zondervan, 1993), 33.

65. Genesis 39:2-4a, 6
66. Genesis 41:38-40
67. See Genesis 22:18
68. See Genesis 48:5
69. Romans 8:28 says, "And we know that God causes everything to work together for the good of those who love God and are called according to his purpose for them."
70. You can find this quote in the *Heart of a Soul Surfer* documentary, at about the twenty-eight-minute mark. Watch it! www .heartofasoulsurfer.com.
71. See Genesis 15:5.
72. See Genesis 17:21.
73. Genesis 17:13
74. Romans 10:12
75. Philippians 3:5b, 6b
76. Acts 6:15
77. Acts 8:3
78. Acts 9:1
79. Acts 9:3-6
80. Acts 9:15-16
81. Proverbs 1:7
82. Luke 1:50
83. Isaiah 43:1b, ESV
84. Genesis 15:1
85. You can find out more about this series and even watch some old episodes at http://www.cbsnews.com/news/everybody-has-a -story-flashbacks/.
86. Matthew 5:45
87. John 16:33. The passage goes on to say, "But take heart, because I have overcome the world."
88. Romans 5:2-5
89. A man from my church in Dallas wrote a detailed article about what Yom Kippur means as part of God's good news. If you'd like to read more about Yom Kippur, you can find that article here: http://www.thevillagechurch.net/sermon/the-gospel-in-the-day -of-atonement/.
90. See Hebrews 10.
91. Romans 8:23-24

lolo MAGAZINE

LOLO Magazine is the ultimate lifestyle experience—your one-stop site for industry buzz, fashion reviews, local shopping hot spots, fitness insights, fresh new recipes, and all-the-rage beauty products. At *LOLO Magazine*, living is more than just dreaming—so get inspired to bring your own dreams to life!

Visit www.lolomag.com to let *LOLO* bring life-style to you.